THE ENIGMA
OF THE
CROSS

THE ENIGMA OF THE CROSS

Alister McGrath

HODDER AND STOUGHTON
LONDON SYDNEY AUCKLAND AUSTRALIA

Acknowledgments

The author and publisher are grateful to the following sources for permission to use copyright material:

Four lines from 'Little Gidding' from 'Four Quartets', taken from *Collected Poems 1909–1962* by T. S. Eliot. Faber and Faber Limited.

Two lines ('we had the experience') from 'Dry Salvages' from 'Four Quartets', taken from *Collected Poems 1909–1962* by T. S. Eliot. Faber and Faber Limited.

Two lines ('The only wisdom') from 'East Coker', from 'Four Quartets' taken from *Collected Poems 1909–1962* by T. S. Eliot. Faber and Faber Limited

All biblical quotations are the author's own translation unless otherwise stated.

British Library Cataloguing in Publication Data

McGrath, Alister E.
  The enigma of the cross.
  1. Jesus Christ—Crucifixion
  I. Title
  232.9'63   BT450

  ISBN 0 340 41064 7

CONTENTS

FOREWORD

It is salutary to recall that it was the Cross on the Hill rather than the Sermon on the Mount which produced the impact of Christianity upon the world. This message was offensive to Jew and Greek alike, yet the early church held on to it, eventually to out-live and out-think its pagan environment. Throughout Acts and the Pauline corpus, we encounter the intensity of this simple message, and recall that in the post-resurrection discourse at Emmaus the risen Christ himself explained that this message held together the entire Old Testament preparation through Moses and the prophets: it had to be this way, of necessity. When the disciples saw this truth their hearts burnt within them.

It was a later disciple who restored this truth to Christendom. After fifteen hundred years of continuing involvement with the secular powers, and deepening identification with secular culture, the church found itself addressed by an obscure and intense monk to face again the truth of what he called the 'theology of the cross', and to accept the consequences. The only theology which would release the church from its own self-imposed intellectualised scholasticism, the only theology to set the church up not as the wisdom of man but under the power of God, was the word of the cross.

It is important to see how Luther did this. Following the commotion of the publication of his theses against indulgences in 1517, and against scholastic theology, he was invited to address his fellow Augustinian monks at their triennial chapter at Heidelberg in 1518. Here, free of controversy and addressing godly men, he explained his theology of the cross.

He did so by explaining the significance and the meaning of God's confrontation of Moses, recorded in Exodus 33, where Moses begs to be made *certain* of God's presence in his mission, or at least to see and know that God is there. It is a despairing cry for faith. God tells Moses that he shall never see his face, only his back: and that is his only certainty. Luther interprets 'the back parts of God' to mean the despair and the anguish of the absence of God, of being forsaken by God, of the contradictions of life: in short, the cross. But it is of decisive importance to see what Luther taught was not that God is somehow there, *in spite of* defeat, sorrow, pain, humiliation, anguish, failure, sin and death. Not at all! He taught that God himself confronts us in person and makes his presence near *in and through* defeat, sorrow, pain, humiliation, anguish, failure, sin and death. The 'contrary things' of failure, sin and death constitute the raw material which God transforms into his own self in the human heart. God reveals himself through a contrary form. It is the back of God which is revealed – but it *is* God, and not another. To learn this is to learn Christ. To know this at first hand, to have the enigma of the cross so explained, is to have tapped the very source and spring of the Christian faith.

The value of this book is not only that Dr McGrath indicates the truth of Luther's position when he offered the church a *re*formation of the *de*formation she had suffered over the centuries: he takes the decisive step of indicating what this means for the faith of the individual believer and the life of the church, which in any and every age, at any and all times, is in a continuing state of needing reformation. He shows himself keenly aware of the contemporary theological scene, as well as of scientific thinking, and makes the decisive contribution to present-day academic thinking, that Christian faith is not about ideas and concepts, but is an encounter with the living God, an encounter which takes place through the death and resurrection of Jesus Christ. We have the cross here and now, the resurrection on the last day: God's back now, God's face then. We are not handling ideas, we are being handled by a person.

To a world which has lost its belief in God, to clergy and laity who long to believe again, to people who know only the ache of the absence of God but never his presence, this book offers a great deal. Based on sound learning which never obtrudes, and fired by a firm faith and a love of the church, the very truth of its argument illuminates the mind and refreshes the soul.

This book offers a timely, and even a prophetic, word to the church today, and a saving and strengthening word to those who have little or no faith, yet seek some answer to the riddle of life. It would make a splendid Lenten study: it will certainly strengthen faith and restore hope. I commend it warmly, and leave the reader with a thought from Luther's *Heidelberg Disputation* (1518):

> The cross teaches us to believe in hope even when there is no hope. The wisdom of the cross is hidden deeply in a profound mystery. In fact, there is no other way to heaven than taking up the cross of Christ. On account of this we must beware that the active life with its good works, and the contemplative life with its speculations, do not lead us astray. Both are most attractive and give peace of mind, but for that very reason hide real dangers, unless they are tempered by the cross and disturbed by adversaries. The cross is the surest path of all. Blessed is the man who understands this truth.

Professor James Atkinson
Director, Centre for Reformation studies
University of Sheffield

BY WAY OF EXPLANATION

'A picture held us captive', wrote the Austrian philosopher Ludwig Wittgenstein as he discussed the remarkable power of symbols over the way in which we think and try to understand the world. Our understanding of the world revolves around 'pictures' which seem to hold the key by which the mystery of life may be unlocked.

At the centre of the Christian faith lies a picture. Christian art and architecture, literature and hymns, are dominated by the symbol of the cross. A symbol, however, both invites and demands thought and reflection. What are we to make of this symbol? What does it tell us about God and the world, or about our nature and ultimate destiny? Why is it that at the centre of a faith in a loving God lies a symbol of death and despair – the dreadful picture of a man dying through crucifixion?

The cross is indeed an enigma, something difficult to understand, but charged with meaning for those who despair of the apparent pointlessness of human existence, who feel lost in the world and overwhelmed by its concerns and anxieties. The cross is also a powerful challenge to the complacency of the Christian church. The cross continually raises questions for the church, which dares to call itself 'Christian' after the one who was crucified and rose again, and yet seems to prefer to look for the grounds of its identity and relevance elsewhere than in the crucified Christ.

The present book is an attempt to unfold the crucial enigma which lies at the heart of the Christian faith, and indicate its meaning for the life of the church. It falls into two parts. The first is concerned with establishing the centrality of the cross to Christianity. It is shown that the cross cannot be marginalised within, let alone eliminated from, the Christian faith. The identity and relevance of Christianity are both irrevocably tied up with the crucified Christ. The second part is concerned with exploring the meaning of the enigma with which we are confronted in the crucified Christ. All too often the cross is relegated to one small area of Christian doctrine – how Christ gained re-demption for us (soteriology) – whereas in fact it stamps an indelible and decisive impression upon every facet of the Christian faith. What does it mean for our understanding of God, of ourselves and of the world? How does it cast light on the doubt and anxiety we encounter in our lives as Christians, on the contradictions we are faced with in our existence? How does it help us wrestle with questions of doctrine, ethics or spirituality? How does it relate to human suffering and oppression? In all these matters the enigma of the cross provides the key by which an *authentically Christian* approach to these issues may be gained.

A word of explanation concerning how this book came to be written may help the reader understand it better.

Some years ago I wrote a book dealing with the origins of Martin Luther's celebrated 'theology of the cross'. Although many of the ideas which Luther developed were not new, his genius lay in the way in which he brought them together to create one of the most powerful and radical understandings of the identity and relevance of Christianity ever known. Just as a master smith might take a block of iron and forge it into a double-edged sword, so Luther took existing ideas and forged them into a reforming and renewing theology on the basis of which the church might take its stand against the world. Luther drew together the hard-won insights of many years of theological and spiritual agonising, welding them into the single weapon of the 'theology of the cross'. As I wrote that book I became increasingly aware of the remarkable power and relevance of the ideas Luther developed and decided that, when time permitted, I would try to present these ideas in a form suitable for our own times.

Although Luther's 'theology of the cross' was virtually ignored for the first four centuries of its existence, there has recently been a growing realisation that this exciting and challenging means of understanding the way in which God is at work in his world may well form the basis for the recovery of both the identity and relevance of Christianity in the years which lie ahead. Every now and then one generation of Christians rediscovers an aspect of the Christian faith which had been neglected or dismissed as useless by previous generations – and it seems that the 'theology of the cross' illustrates exactly this trend. What one generation dismissed or overlooked has been gratefully recovered and appropriated by another.

'The cross puts everything to the test.' For Luther, Christian thinking about God comes to an abrupt halt at the foot of the cross. The very existence of the cross, and of the crucified Christ, forces us to make a crucial decision: Will we look for God somewhere else, or will we make the cross, and the crucified Christ, the basis of our thought about God?

The cross marks a dead end for much thinking about God, and opens the way to an authentically *Christian* understanding of the 'God and father of our Lord Jesus Christ'. It is both the foundation and the criterion of the life and faith of the Christian believer and the Christian church. The cross presents us with a riddle, with an enigma – and the solution of that riddle holds the key to the Christian understanding of the nature and purposes of God, of human nature and destiny. It is a crucial enigma, for the identity and relevance of the Christian faith are ultimately bound up with it, and cannot be separated from it. And it is to wrestling with that enigma that we now turn.

I wish to thank James Atkinson, Paul Avis, Richard Bauckham, Tony Clark, Andrew Hodder-Williams and Nigel Taylor for reading earlier versions of this work, and making invaluable comments upon it, and particularly Professor Atkinson for contributing the foreword.

Part One

The centrality of the cross

1 THE CROSS AS THE BASIS OF CHRISTIANITY

God, the God I love and worship, reigns in sorrow
on the Tree,
Broken, bleeding, but unconquered, very God of
God to me.

G. A. Studdert-Kennedy

History, we are told, is irreversible, and we cannot undo her handiwork. Part of that history is the fact that Christian faith was created, aroused and shaped by the crucifixion and resurrection of Jesus Christ – a pattern of events which lay beyond its control, and to which it could only respond in increasing wonder and amazement as its implications were unfolded. Here, it seemed, was none other than God stooping to enter and redeem the tragic history of his creation. It was the action of God to which a reaction was demanded.

In the crucifixion and resurrection of Jesus Christ is something 'given', something over which we have no control. We may accept it, and respond to it, attempting to work out its implications for our understanding of God and the world; we may reject it, and base this understanding upon something else. But only the former may lay claim to be an authentically *Christian* approach.

As we shall emphasise time and time again in the present work, the word 'Christian' cannot be appropriated by anyone who wishes to make some sort of statement about God based upon whatever foundation he may choose –

authentically *Christian* statements about God are based upon the crucified and risen Christ.

Christian theology ought therefore not to be about wrestling with ideas, but about wrestling with the living God. There is every danger that the academic theologian will be trapped in what Karl Barth called an 'idolatry of concepts' as he attempts to wrestle with the way in which ideas and concepts relate to each other. But the Christian faith is not first and foremost about ideas or concepts, even though it may give rise to them. At its heart lies not an idea or a concept but an event in human history. The theologian cannot be allowed to retreat from history into his private world of ideas and close the door after him. For something *happened*, not in the world of ideas, but in human history. And in that historical event, some recognised that they were being addressed by the living God himself, speaking to them and calling them to faith in him.

The Christian faith stands or falls with the identification and involvement of God himself with the crucified Christ. So central is the cross to Christianity that if God is *not* revealed in and involved with it, Christian faith must be recognised as a delusion – a profound and deeply satisfying delusion, it is true, but a delusion none the less.

When the New Testament speaks of 'God' it does not have an anonymous concept in mind, but it directs our attention and our concentration to a point, to a moment in history. From its beginning to its end the New Testament directs us to the crucified Christ who is now risen. Here is no idea, no concept, which we can kick about in discussion groups or seminar rooms – here is the living God who makes himself available for our acceptance or rejection in the crucified Christ.

The criterion of what is Christian and what is not is the cross of Jesus Christ, the crucial enigma which distinguishes the peculiarly Christian way of looking at human existence and experience from all other viewpoints.

This is not to say that other viewpoints do not exist, nor even to suggest that they are *wrong* – it is simply to say that the point of reference for deciding which theological statements are Christian and which are not is 'given' to us in the crucified Christ. The cross of Christ is the point of reference for Christian faith; Christian faith is based upon it and judged by it – in short, the cross is the foundation and the criterion of Christian faith. Christian theology, Christian worship and Christian ethics are essentially nothing other than an attempt to explore and develop the meaning and implications of the crucified Christ in every area of life. Christianity does not concern one small aspect of our lives, leaving the rest unaffected – it is about bringing our entire existence, the way we think and the way we act, into line with the model given to us in the crucified and risen Christ. Far from being just the basis of a 'private' or 'interiorised' religion, the cross opens the way to a radical and authentically *Christian* approach to ethics and politics.

The crisis of confidence within Christianity

Within the western world, particularly Europe and North America, the Christian church appears to be undergoing a double crisis of confidence.

Many have lost confidence in the *relevance* of the Christian gospel to contemporary society, and sought solace in social work and other spheres of action which were thought to be 'relevant' in a way which the Christian faith was not.

Others, realising that Christianity had a distinctive contribution to make to social debate, attempted to show the relevance of the gospel by writing learned papers on matters such as 'The Theology of Housing Subsidies' – and by their theological confusion and incoherence showed up the second major crisis facing Christianity today: The lack of any real understanding of the peculiar *identity* of Christian faith, which prevented any distinctively *Christian* insights being brought to bear on the matters which they wished to discuss.

The question of whether Christianity has any distinctive and decisive insights which ought to be heard in the modern world presupposes some sort of agreement about what Christianity is really all about. Even in liberal western-style democracies there is a growing realisation within the churches that Christianity can no longer be identified with liberal attitudes (whether contemporary or classical) but concerns something far deeper – something which may even in the end come into conflict with the values of the societies in which they exist.

The relevance of Christianity to the modern world is closely tied up with the question of the fundamental nature of Christianity itself. Without a clear sense of its identity and purpose Christianity will have little relevance in the eyes of the world. Similarly, the realisation of the relevance of Christianity for the world casts light on the identity of Christian faith and Christian theology. Thus Martin Kähler could speak of mission as being 'the mother of theology'. In other words, *proclaiming* and *defending* Christianity in the face of other outlooks on life (whether secular or religious) gives us important insights into the nature of Christianity itself, as well as the adequacy of certain interpretations of it. An example will help bring this point out.

The German-American theologian Paul Tillich developed an approach to Christianity which involved the virtual elimination of the idea of a personal God, as traditionally understood, making it impossible (or at least very difficult) to make sense of things like a 'personal relationship with God' or prayer and worship – all integral parts of the way most Christians think about and practise their faith. An American theologian, a disciple of Tillich, went to work in Uganda for some time and found himself one day in a village square. On learning that he was interested in theology, one of the villagers called the village community together and announced that their visitor was going to 'tell them all about Jesus Christ'. As they waited expectantly the American theologian found himself at a loss for words. As he later reflected on his experience: 'I realised that Tillich just wasn't going to cut any ice there!'

Historically, it is certainly true that 'mission is the mother of theology' – perhaps not all of Christian theology, but certainly a large part of it. As the early church began its explosion into the Mediterranean world of the first and second centuries, it found itself obliged to defend itself in the face of opposition from religious beliefs – both Jewish and Greek – already established in those areas. Thus the early Christians were forced to consider what distinguished their beliefs from those they encountered, and thus to clarify exactly what it was that they believed. They had no doubts about the *relevance* of what they proclaimed – the difficulty they encountered was preserving its *identity* in the new situation in which they found themselves. Realising that the relevance of Christianity depended upon maintaining its identity, they made every attempt possible to uphold the distinction between their beliefs and those in the world around them. Nor is this something which was true only in the first two centuries. The history of Christian missions in India and Africa shows exactly the same principles in operation in the eighteenth, nineteenth and twentieth centuries. Christianity's relevance depends upon maintaining its identity.

A similar point has been made by the poet T. S. Eliot in the following lines:

> We had the experience, but missed the meaning;
> But approach to the meaning restored the experience.
>
> *Dry Salvages*

The experience which Christianity proclaims as a genuine possibility is tied up with the question of its meaning – and the two are inseparable. One of the main reasons why the early church fathers became so involved in questions of doctrine was because they realised that the continuing relevance of Christianity to their own generation, and for countless generations to come, was dependent upon preserving certain crucial insights, all too easily lost. Experience and meaning, relevance and identity, are mutually dependent. The crisis of relevance and the crisis of identity are related – indeed, they may even be said to be the same, viewed from two different standpoints. The former is the *external* crisis, the way in which Christianity is viewed by those who stand outside it; the latter is the *internal* crisis, the way in which Christianity is viewed by those inside it.

The solution to these crises lies in a recovery of the identity of Christianity in the crucifixion and resurrection of Jesus Christ. The thing that is distinctive and characteristic about Christian faith and Christian theology, giving it simultaneously both its identity and relevance, is the cross of Christ. The death and resurrection of Jesus Christ marks the beginning of a specifically Christian outlook on exist- ence, embracing matters of doctrine, ethics and spirituality, and guaranteeing its continued relevance for man.

So long as human beings walk the face of the earth knowing that they must die, and seeking a key to the riddle of human nature and destiny, Christianity will continue to confront them with a crucial enigma, whose unravelling casts light upon, and gives hope to, the human situation. Having lost confidence in the relevance and reality of this central feature of its message, the western church has tried other remedies for its crisis of relevance, only to find them wanting. Perhaps it is time it returned to reclaim its distinc- tive insights, to which it is heir, allowing the crucified Christ to step into a church to which he has been a stranger for so long.

The cross is deeply embedded at every level of the Christian tradition, both as the primal event of faith and the symbolic expression of that same faith in Christian art and architecture, hymns and liturgy. It is time for Christianity to break free from the social and cultural prison in which it has been for so long a secret prisoner, and return to that primal event of faith, to discover in it a liberating, radical and critical faith, charged with a vitality far exceeding the insipid endorsement of liberal cultural values which passes as 'Christianity' in much of the western world.

'Back to the sources!' was the battle cry of humanists and reformers alike in the sixteenth century, and we would do well to heed them, returning to the source of Christian faith and reappropriating it – the cross of Jesus Christ. In the remainder of this book, we will be exploring how this might be done, and what it might lead to, as we take the words of Goethe with the seriousness which they so clearly deserve:

> What you received as an inheritance,
> Make now your own, in order to use it!

The story of the cross

History, we are being told more and more often, tells stories. Christianity also tells a story. It is a long and complex story which tells of creation and redemption, and of the mysterious way in which God is present and active in his world. The story has enormous dramatic appeal at some points, as when the children of Israel are led out from bondage in Egypt to begin the pilgrimage into the promised land. It is the story of a faithful God and his people, whom he called into being. It is, however, a story which quickly gathers momentum with the arrival of John the Baptist, proclaiming the imminent arrival of the one who was greater than he, and with the inauguration of the ministry of Jesus Christ.

That great story, perhaps the greatest story the world has ever told, has as its centre and its focal point the crucifixion and resurrection of Jesus Christ. Up to that point the story has at times been unclear and apparently pointless – from that point onwards the story gains a new vitality, dynamism and relevance. The story is that of the man who was crucified, apparently rejected and abandoned by God, executed by his own people, and given up for lost even by those who had been closest to him. The story is that of the man who was raised from the dead, recognised by those who had known him, and acknowledged by those who had never known him during his lifetime. The story of the man who was crucified and raised underlies much of the material in the New Testament, being recounted explicitly at points, and hinted at in others.

This story has been at the heart of the worship of the

Christian church throughout the ages. Although Christians have found themselves unable to agree on the name of the form of worship which some call 'Holy Communion', others 'the Eucharist', and others 'the Mass', there is universal agreement that this central form of worship at the very least commemorates, re-enacts and recalls to memory the death and resurrection of Jesus Christ, and the benefits which these are understood to bring to those who believe in him. Christians simply do not revere Jesus Christ as a dead rabbi of the past, but worship him as the present, living, risen Lord.

Stories illuminate and transform our human experience and existence. One of the best-known stories is that of the liberation of the children of Israel from slavery in Egypt through the act of God. Every age has its Egypt, its force of oppression, just as every age has its children of Israel who long to be free. The black slaves in the American deep south and their successors in the civil rights movement saw that this story applied to them: *they* were Israel; *they* were in bondage; *they* hoped for freedom. The story spoke of deliverance from a more powerful oppressor, against all the apparent odds; it spoke of hope in the midst of a desperate, hopeless and helpless situation; it gave birth to faith in the possibility of redemption, of liberation, and a determination to work towards that end. As Martin Luther King observed in his famous sermon 'The Death of Evil upon the Seashore', 'without such faith, man's highest dreams will pass silently to the dust'. Because the story spoke of a situation characteristic of the human predicament, it retains its appeal: every age will have its Egypt and its children of Israel, its oppressors and its oppressed; every age will see the hope of liberation cherished by those held in bondage, who will see their own situation reflected in and illuminated by the exodus narrative, and gain insight and hope by doing so.

So it is also with the story of the crucifixion and resurrection of Jesus. The story takes up and develops themes already found in the exodus story, just as many great novels or symphonies contain initial statements of a theme, followed by its subsequent development. The story here is that of life being gained through death, of strength being displayed in apparent weakness, of hope in the face of total despair. It is the story of our last and greatest enemy, our own mortality and future death, being conquered and disarmed. And just as we may see our own situation reflected in the exodus story, so we see our own situation reflected in the story of the crucifixion and resurrection of Jesus Christ. Our own secret doubts and apparent failure, our fear of death, our sense of hopelessness and helplessness, to name but some themes which we shall soon be exploring – all are illuminated, interpreted and transformed by the crucified Christ. The story comes to have a powerful *existential* significance.

The realisation of the existential significance of a fact, or an event, can be devastating. I can still remember the time when I managed to reason from a general truth (everyone must die) to the particular truth that *I* must die, and the sense of anxiety that came with this realisation. This was not a truth which I could pretend affected everyone but me, or something which I could entirely overlook. While it was convenient to ignore it at times, the simple and disconcerting fact of my mortality was something which I realised I would have to come to terms with. No longer was I talking in terms of the general biological fact of death, but of the termination of my personal and individual existence.

My realisation of my mortality could thus be said to assume *existential* significance – in other words, I realised that it was something relevant to the way I understood myself and the world, and forced me to raise some difficult questions. The same is true of the crucified Christ, who is charged with existential significance for the human situation. The story of crucifixion and resurrection, of life through death, of recovery through loss, has many points of contact with human experience of grief, loss, despair and anxiety concerning the meaning of life. At some point we realise that this story applies to us – that it is we who have been crucified and raised with Christ, as Paul puts it (e.g. Galatians 2:20; 6:14).

The Christian answers to 'ultimate questions' – questions about the meaning of life, the threat of death and extinction, the seeming hopelessness of the human situation – are grounded in the story of God's dealings with us, which culminates in and is focused upon the crucified and risen Christ. The events of the first Good Friday and Easter Day are like a lens through which we know God, ourselves and the world, and at the same time know ourselves to be judged by another. The cross brings these central concerns to a focus, allowing us to see them in a certain light and from a certain aspect, and thus to evaluate them. What ought to be distinctive about the Christian's insights is not merely the nature of these insights themselves but also the manner in which they are derived. For the Christian 'the cross alone is our theology' (Luther).

Stories need to be interpreted, and one of the easiest ways of interpreting a story is to retell it. Retelling a story means leaving out bits which aren't important and highlighting those which are of central importance. And in the retelling of the story of God's dealings with us the Christian tradition has constantly identified the death and resurrection of Jesus Christ as the climax of that story, holding the key to its entire meaning. In fact the Christian story just cannot be told without the narrative of the crucifixion and resurrection. In Paul's shorthand version of the Christian faith we find the crucifixion-resurrection story identified as central: 'I delivered to you as of first importance what I also received, that Christ died for our sins in accordance with the scriptures, that he was buried, that he was raised on the third day in accordance with the scriptures' (1 Corinthians 15:3–4 RSV).

To make this point clearer, let us look at the way in which Christians worship. Many Christians (such as Lutherans, Anglicans, Methodists and Roman Catholics) use a liturgical form of worship in which a fixed pattern of words is used in congregational worship. These fixed forms of words are based directly or indirectly upon forms used in the earliest period of the Christian tradition and embody very early authentic insights into the nature and identity of

Christianity. In the case of what is often referred to as the 'eucharistic liturgy' (in other words, the form of words used for the communion service) we find the entire Christian story summarised in a few sentences. It has been *retold* in such a way as to bring out what is really important and to prevent us from being distracted by matters of lesser importance. And the crucial elements of that story are the death and resurrection of Jesus Christ.

Sometimes we hear people speaking about an *authoritative* performance of a Shakespeare play such as *Macbeth*. Or we may hear someone suggest that a certain conductor's version of a Mozart symphony is *authoritative*. What do they mean by this? Usually what is meant is that the performance of the play or symphony seems to bring out its full meaning in a way that no other does and that other versions of the same play or symphony are called into question or altogether overshadowed. When we want to see that play or hear that symphony at its best, learning to appreciate its character as fully as we can, we look for an *authoritative* performance. An authoritative performance of *Macbeth*, for example, allows us to gain insights into its characters which we might not have gained with another version. An authoritative performance allows us to begin to distinguish what is central, what is *essential*, about a work from what is peripheral and not very important. It establishes the norm by which subsequent performances are judged, challenging their interpretation of their material and their right to perform it in any other way.

In much the same way, we can talk about an *authoritative* retelling of the Christian story in the liturgy of the Christian church. This authoritative retelling has the full weight of two thousand years of Christian experience behind it and it unequivocally identifies the crucifixion and resurrection of Jesus Christ as the primal event of faith, the fulcrum about which the Christian faith and Christian experience alike turn. It allows us to gain insights which we might otherwise be denied (for example, by those who retell the Christian story to make Jesus out to be nothing more than a rabbi or a peddler of religious ideas) and it allows us to distinguish what is *essential* to the understanding of the story (the cross and resurrection) from what is merely peripheral (e.g., whether Jesus was a vegetarian).

Every other retelling of the Christian story is over-shadowed and called into question by the way in which Christians have worshipped Jesus Christ down the ages. Christians do not mourn Jesus as a dead rabbi, but worship him as the risen Lord, rejoicing in the fact that the one who was crucified has now been raised to glory. And *any* theology which is unable to reproduce or incorporate the centrality of the cross and resurrection into the way in which Christians have worshipped must have its claim to call itself 'Christian' called into question.

As we shall emphasise later in this work, a study of the Christian understanding of the nature of God or of the identity and significance of Jesus Christ cannot be under-taken in *complete* isolation from the Christian tradition! And that tradition points to the crucified and risen Christ as the primal event upon which Christian faith is based, and hence upon which Christian insights must be based and judged. This is not necessarily to say that this tradition is right or wrong in doing so – but it is unquestionably to say that it is unequivocally *Christian* in doing so.

The word of the cross and Paul

According to his own account, and several in Acts which are probably based upon this, Paul's Christian experience began with a remarkable revelation of the glory of the risen Christ (Acts 9:3; 22:6,11; 26:13; 1 Corinthians 9:1; 15:8; Galatians 1:16). It is clear that the great theme of the triumph of the risen Lord Jesus over death continued to be a central theme of his thought, and probably also his exten-sive missionary preaching. It might therefore be expected that Paul's thought should be triumphalist, centred upon the great themes of victory, triumph and exaltation – that of Jesus Christ here and now, and that of the Christian at the last day. In fact, this is simply not the case. Indeed, several

modern commentators on 1 Corinthians have suggested
that Paul was engaged in combating precisely this sort of
triumphalism at Corinth.

If any aspect of the story of Jesus Christ may be said to
dominate Paul's thought, it is not the resurrection, but
the cross. The sheer *oddness* of this fact is often overlooked.
Long before Paul wrote, the Christian tradition – in
theological reflection and liturgical confessions – had
recognised the death of Jesus on the cross as the saving
event, and established that the enigma of the cross, far from
representing a totally disastrous event marking the end of
the career of Jesus and a 'Christianity' based upon his
teaching, was nothing less than *the* event of divine redemption and the beginning of the authentically Christian way
of understanding God and his world. Nevertheless, Paul
developed this approach with a critical sharpness which
consolidated the centrality of the cross to the understanding of the early Christian church.

Perhaps the most powerful statement of the 'theology
of the cross' in the Pauline epistles may be found in 1
Corinthians 1:18–2:5. This remarkable passage bristles
with astonishing insights into the significance and relevance of the cross, with the resurrection being virtually
ignored. Why should Paul concentrate his attention upon
the cross when his own experience was that of the risen and
glorified Christ?

Many modern studies of the church at Corinth have
suggested that the Corinthian Christians had become
caught up in a form of triumphalism which had a one-sided
emphasis upon the exaltation of Jesus Christ. The frequent
references to 'wisdom' and 'knowledge' in 1 Corinthians
are usually held to indicate that the Corinthian church
had adopted some form of gnosticism – a religious system
based upon some form of 'knowledge' only available to
'enlightened' individuals. Just as Christ has ascended into
heaven, so believers were thought to have ascended with
him in mind to gain knowledge of the heavenly realms.

Against this wild unhistorical speculation Paul sets a
historical fact: the cross. The cross brings such speculation

down to earth once more; in the place of the ethereal truths of the spiritual realm, which may be discerned only by those with 'knowledge' or 'wisdom', the cross confronts us with something concrete. For Paul, knowledge, wisdom and power are indeed revealed by God to the Christian believer – but they are revealed in the dreadful and scandalous spectacle of the crucified Christ. This is the point at which theological speculation must begin. Against intellectual or gnostic 'wisdom', Paul sets a concrete historical event, discernible to all, and not just a select élite. Faith has its basis firmly established in human history. But it is far more than just theological speculation which Paul bases upon the cross – his whole understanding of Christian existence and experience is grounded in the fate of the crucified Christ.

For Paul, death and life, weakness and strength, suffering and glory, wisdom and folly, sorrow and joy, are all interwoven in the remarkable event of the cross. Paul's understanding of both the mission of Jesus Christ and Christian existence itself is dominated by such cross-centred themes of life in death and strength in weakness. The full force of Paul's insights is missed if we interpret him as teaching that we can have life *despite* death and strength *despite* weakness: for Paul, the remarkable meaning of the enigma of the cross is that life comes *through* death and strength *through* weakness. The enigma of the cross symbolises the remarkable and paradoxical way in which God works out the salvation of those he loves – an enigma which is supremely demonstrated in the crucified and risen Christ, but which bears direct relevance to Paul's understanding of Christian existence.

The Corinthian Christians were, in effect, behaving as if the age to come were already consummated and the full power of the resurrection life had already broken into the existence of the believer. By emphasising the centrality and dominance of the cross, Paul draws attention to the dialectic of the cross and resurrection in Christian experience – there is a tension between the 'here and now' of the cross and the 'there and then' of the resurrection. In Paul's thought the resurrection remains a future event, a 'not yet' which illuminates and transforms the present without breaking into it with full force. The Christian is forced to concede that he must live and struggle with the reality of his earthly situation, while continually looking forward to the future resurrection and interpreting the present in its light.

For Paul, to take the cross of Christ with full seriousness is to take with equal seriousness the remainder of our existence here on earth, before being raised with Christ in glory. To be a theologian of the cross is thus to remain rooted in the specific historical situation in which we find ourselves, neither dismissing it as irrelevant in the light of the future resurrection nor treating it as if it alone constituted the bounds of our existence.

The theology of the cross recognises the tensions in Christian existence, exposing them for what they really are and allowing us a realistic sense of perspective into our situation. The cross and resurrection demonstrate and illuminate the genuine tension between the 'here and now' and 'there and then' in the life of the individual believer and the church and prohibit the elimination of this tension if an authentically *Christian* understanding of that existence is to result.

Careful study of the New Testament texts suggests that the death of Jesus Christ upon the cross was initially regarded as an impenetrable enigma, a dark riddle, which was only solved through the resurrection. The event of the cross is given its meaning by the resurrection (Acts 2:31–33; 1 Corinthians 2:7–8). Thus at points Paul treats the resurrection as a demonstration that Jesus is indeed the Son of God (Romans 1:3–4) – something which the cross initially seemed to deny (Galatians 3:13b). There is therefore a tendency, almost certainly found at Corinth and not un-known even today, to view the cross simply as one stage in the progress from Christ's earthly life to his exaltation at the right hand of God. It is just one of many stages in that progress, and cannot be regarded as particularly important in itself. The Christian, it is argued, ought to be concerned with the risen, rather than with the crucified, Christ.

The death of Jesus on the cross is overshadowed by his exaltation.

Although these observations have some truth, they lack a crucial insight which Paul so clearly perceived. For Paul, the death of Christ upon the cross raised a number of serious questions to which the resurrection gave answers: How could something so scandalous (to the Jew) and foolish (to the Greeks) possess universal saving significance? How could God identify himself with one who was so clearly abandoned by God? Does total and radical obedience to God lead only to a humiliating and insignificant death? Is this the dreadful and pointless fate of everyone who treads the path which Christ trod before them?

Questions such as these are raised with some force by the cross. In the light of the resurrection of Jesus Christ, these questions may be answered, giving a 'theology of the cross': God's strength is revealed *through* (not *despite!*) the weakness of the cross; life is gained *through* (not *despite!*) death, and so forth. But the crucial insight which Paul brings out is this: It is Christ alone who has been raised, and our resurrection remains in the future.

It is therefore the cross, the culmination of the earthly ministry of Jesus Christ, which remains the key to our earthly Christian existence. The cross is, to be sure, interpreted in the light of the resurrection, so that we now have the key to this crucial enigma – but it is the cross, interpreted in the light of the resurrection, which must remain the key to our understanding of this world and our destiny within it. Christian existence in general, and Christian *discipleship* in particular, are governed by the cross.

To give the resurrection priority over the crucifixion is to retreat from the realities of this world into the 'heavenly realms', developing an idealistic view of the world and our place in it which bears little relation to the situation in which we find ourselves here and now. Knowing that the one who was crucified was raised by God allows us to see the present world in a different light and gives us certain crucial insights into the nature of weakness, suffering, persecution and death – but it does not allow us to pass from the present into the heavenly world. We remain where we are – but are allowed to see things in the light of the cross and resurrection.

This side of the resurrection, but viewed in the light of that resurrection, the cross remains the model 'given' to the believer, by which he may make sense of the profound contradictions he encounters in his Christian experience and existence. Paul himself carefully excludes the theory that we share the fullness of the resurrection life *here and now*, by insisting that it is a future reality. Christian existence here and now is an enigma, just as the cross was – and the latter allows us to make sense of the former. Cross and resurrection are indeed closely linked, but in such a way as to exclude the possibility of Christians detaching themselves from the realities of the present situation. There is a dialectic, a tension, between cross and resurrection in Christian experience.

The cross is a key by which the ambiguities of human existence may be unlocked, casting light on the situation in which the Christian now finds himself in the world. Knowing that the one who was crucified was raised, and knowing that he himself has been crucified with Christ, the believer may make the crucified Christ the guiding principle of his life. He is freed from the anxieties of the world, in that the cross discloses to him that anxiety is unwarranted in the light of the resurrection. As Paul himself puts it, in a remarkable statement: 'Far be it from me to glory except in the cross of our Lord Jesus Christ, by which the world has been crucified to me, and I to the world' (Galatians 6:14 RSV). For the believer, the knowledge that he will share in both the 'sufferings of the present age' (Romans 8:18) and in the glory of the risen Christ means that the anxieties and concerns of the world are put to an end. The world is crucified, to use Paul's daring phrase.

We shall explore and develop Paul's logic of the cross later in this work. For the moment, we are mainly concerned with showing that the cross is a central element of Paul's understanding of the Christian life, and cannot be eliminated or ignored. Our attention now shifts to the gospels themselves. It is on the basis of the gospel accounts that some critics have argued that the cross may be regarded as a peripheral, inessential, element of the Christian faith.

The cross in the synoptic gospels

It is often pointed out, particularly by those who wish to treat Christianity as if it were totally, or mainly, about obeying the ethical teachings of Jesus Christ, that the first three gospels (Matthew, Mark and Luke, usually referred to as the 'synoptic gospels') devote relatively little space to their accounts of the death and resurrection of Jesus. While this observation is correct, the conclusion drawn on its basis (that the death and resurrection of Jesus are theologically less important than his ethical and religious teaching) is not.

We must remember that the gospels were written at a relatively later stage than Paul's letters, and that both these letters and the earlier Christian tradition which scholars have detected lying behind them tend to treat the cross as the only event in the life of Jesus Christ (apart from the resurrection, of course) which is of decisive importance for the believer. The oldest traditions in the New Testament are those concerning the death of Jesus on the cross, and the significance which this has for believers.

I would remind you, brothers, of the gospel which I preached to you, which you also received, by which also you stand, and through which you are saved; I ask you to note with what form of words I preached the gospel to you . . . For, first of all, I handed on to you that which I also received, namely that Christ died for our sins according to the scriptures, and that he was buried and that according to the scriptures he was raised on the third day.

(1 Corinthians 15:1–4)

It is clear that Paul is passing on (note the solemn 'tradition' language) to his readers something of crucial importance which had been passed on to him – the priority of the death and resurrection of Jesus Christ, and its relevance for believers. Paul didn't invent this understanding of the significance of Jesus' death – it was passed on to him by others, almost certainly representing one of the oldest and most cherished Christian insights concerning the destiny of Jesus Christ.

While it is not quite true to say that the gospels are 'passion narratives with extended introductions' (Martin Kähler), it is nevertheless evident that the passion narratives are to be regarded as the climax of the gospels. The evangelists assemble the tradition concerning Jesus in such a way that the shadow of the cross is projected over his entire ministry. Already in Jesus' preaching, teaching and actions may be seen clues concerning his identity, and hence the potential significance of his death. This was no ordinary man who was crucified, and his death has no ordinary significance. The gospel accounts of Jesus' ministry – what he said and did, the impression which he created among the people – confirm and consolidate what the first Christians already knew on the basis of their reflection upon the meaning of the resurrection: that this man who had died upon the cross was indeed the Son of God.

There is a real danger that the emphasis placed upon the cross and resurrection (for example, by Paul) may lead to these being understood as 'mythic symbols' – in other words, that both the cross and resurrection are abstracted from their real historical context. The gospel narratives prohibit this tendency by emphasising that we are dealing with the death and resurrection of a real historical individual – Jesus of Nazareth. We are talking about the crucified and risen Jesus, the same Jesus whom people knew as 'the carpenter, the son of Mary and brother of James and Joses and Judas and Simon' (Mark 6:3 RSV). To encounter the crucified Christ is not just to encounter a dying and rising god, but to encounter a specific human individual with a definite life history. The gospel accounts of the ministry and passion of Jesus of Nazareth allow us to anchor his crucifixion and resurrection in human history, reminding us that we are dealing with a historical event. The cross must not become detached from the history in which it occurred.

In this introductory chapter, we have begun to make the case for recognising the cruciality of the cross for Christian faith. The quest for the identity and relevance of Christianity is intimately linked with the crucified Jesus – so intimately, in fact, that *any* version of Christianity which is unable to accommodate the centrality of the crucified Christ must have its claim to be called 'Christian' challenged. Christianity is not concerned with random thoughts about God or Jesus Christ or human nature and destiny – it is concerned with wrestling with the mysterious living God, as we encounter him in the cross of Jesus Christ. We are forced to deal with God on his own terms, rather than those of our own choosing. As Luther put it, 'true theology and the knowledge of God are in the crucified Christ'.

In the next chapter we shall develop arguments in support of the fundamental contention that the crucified Christ stands at the centre and heart of the Christian faith and that it is the chief function of Christian theology, ethics and spirituality to unfold the implications of the cross for Christian existence. Thought and action alike must centre upon the cross. To begin our discussion of this point, we must ask how our knowledge of God comes about in the first place. And it is to this question that we now turn.

2 THE INESCAPABILITY OF THE CROSS

How do we come to know about God? This deceptively simple question is all too often ignored. It is evident, however, that it is of considerable importance.

One of the more important insights of modern scientific thinking is the recognition that the way in which knowledge is gained has a decisive effect on the nature of the resulting knowledge. For example, if you are dependent upon certain electronic equipment for investigating the structure of the stars, you may find that you are seriously limited in the knowledge you can gain by the equipment itself. All the information you may *want* to have is not available to you, on account of the way you have to get it. A more concrete example will bring this point out.

Up to about the year 1960, our knowledge of the make-up of the surface of the moon was based on collecting information from the light reflected by the moon from the sun. It gave some information, but not very much. Several decades later, samples of the surface material of the moon were brought back for detailed examination, with a considerable increase in our knowledge of the subject as a result. What we had once known indirectly, we now knew directly and much more reliably. The subject of our curiosity (the surface of the moon) hadn't changed – what *had* changed was the way in which we found out about it.

This example illustrates the point which has gained increasing recognition within the natural sciences – what you know about something is largely determined by the way you find out about it. Our knowledge of something may be severely limited or seriously distorted because of the way we come to know about it in the first place. Hopefully, as time goes on, science develops increasingly refined methods of investigation, which means that the limitations placed upon our knowledge, or the distortions within it, are gradually eliminated.

But what about our knowledge of God? How does *that* come about? It will be obvious that there is no parallel within Christianity to the increasingly sophisticated methods of investigation which science may call upon, so there is no way in which we can expect our knowledge of God to suddenly become more exact or more extensive! And that is why we must ask the question: How does our knowledge of God come about in the first place? Because the way in which that knowledge of God comes about will exercise a decisive influence over the nature of that knowledge itself. In short: *What* we know about God is determined by *how* we know it.

How do we know about God?

How does an authentically *Christian* knowledge of God come about? What, if anything, distinguishes the insights of the Christian from those of anyone else? We may begin to answer these questions by considering some of the answers often given to the question of how God may be known.

For some, God is known through nature. The sight of a starlit sky or a beautiful sunset is enough to convince some that at least one god, and possibly several, must have been responsible for bringing about such a delightful spectacle. The same sort of response is often aroused in some on hearing a particularly splendid piece of music – perhaps a Beethoven symphony. The sheer brilliance of the music and the genius of the composer is enough to persuade some that a divinity of some sort lurks behind it.

Others, moved by the way in which the natural world is ordered, argue that the design of the universe points to a creative mind as its origin. When Isaac Newton discovered the mathematical basis of the laws of planetary motion governing the regularity of the universe as it was then known, many came to the conclusion that this remarkable natural regularity pointed to the existence of a celestial mechanic.

This list could, of course, be extended to some length to indicate the variety of manners in which a natural knowledge of God is held to come about, with an equally great variety of 'gods' as a result.

Nevertheless, as is generally known, considerations such as these are suggestive, rather than conclusive, and tell us little about the nature of the god (or gods). As Cicero complained in his famous work *On the Nature of the Gods*, the ideas men derived from nature concerning the nature of the gods were both fragmentary and inconsistent. The astonishing variety of ideas about God or the gods which have developed during human history is an adequate testimony to the inadequacy of this natural 'knowledge' of God. Furthermore, it will be obvious that it is a very idealised approach. Let us develop this point briefly.

A friend of mine once made a journey from Oxford to a city in the north of England. It was a long journey, so he decided to leave Oxford by train at dawn. As he left Oxford he was spellbound by the beauty of the scene: the dreaming spires appeared to be suspended in mist and the landscape was bathed in an almost supernatural glow as the day gradually dawned. To him it seemed evident that there was indeed a creator God, and that his handiwork was quite spectacular. As his journey progressed, however, he began to doubt his dawn insights. The reason for his journey was to visit, for the last time, a close friend who was dying from cancer. As he reflected upon the utterly pointless pain which he knew his young friend was experiencing, and the knowledge that his death was merely a matter of days away, he began to question the way in which he had earlier seen God present in his world. It was the same God-created world that possessed such ethereal beauty at dawn which was causing his friend such pain and torment. Why could he see God in the glorious sunrise and not in the pain and imminent death of his friend? As he reflected he realised that the fault lay with him and not with God – his own preconceptions of beauty prevented him from recognising God's presence with his dying friend. On his return journey he began to develop the idea that God was indeed present in his friend's suffering, just as he was in the sunrise, and that he must learn to see God in the darkest parts of creation, rather than only in the aesthetically pleasing ones.

It is very easy to see God in beautiful landscapes, yet overlook scenes of famine and natural disaster. It is very easy to see God in a work of human art, yet overlook scenes of human brutality and depravity – but it is human beings who are responsible for both. By paying selective attention to only certain parts of nature, a hopelessly idealised view of God results.

If the incoherence and arbitrariness of these 'natural' views of God is to be eliminated, we need to be given something reliable and authoritative upon which we can base our understanding of God. If it is something of our choosing, it will be nothing more than an idol, something which we ourselves have constructed and dared to call 'God'.

Christianity has always insisted that we *need to be told* what to understand by the term 'God', and that God himself establishes the basis on which we may speak about him. We are dealing with a God who reveals himself, who has taken the initiative away from us, who encounters us before we discover him. When we talk about 'revelation', we are expressing the idea that God himself tells us who he is and what he is like. We are expressing the idea that we are somehow *authorised* to speak about God in a particular way. 'God' is not some*thing* we discover, by looking at starry skies or listening to Mozart flute concertos (and ignoring less pleasant aspects of the world), but is some*one* whom we encounter as he moves towards us. God has taken the initiative away from us by providing us with the basis for responsible discussion of his nature and identity, and of the consequences of this crucial encounter with him in the world.

The basis for responsible Christian discussion of God is given to us – not chosen by us! – in the crucified Christ. We are *authorised* to base our discussion of God upon the crucified Christ. To choose anything other than that which is 'given' to us – the crucified Christ – as the normative basis of our knowledge of God is idolatry.

God may indeed be found in beautiful sunsets, in Mozart flute concertos or in the depths of the human soul – but these are not the *norm*. There are – and this point is too important to be overlooked – certain distinctively and authentically *Christian* insights into the nature of God that arise through reflection upon a particular event in which the Christian understands God to have been normatively revealed – the cross and resurrection of Jesus Christ. To look elsewhere for a definitive knowledge of God is potentially to forfeit the right to call oneself 'Christian'. To suggest that authentically Christian insights may be gained from sources other than the cross – such as sunsets or symphonies – is to retreat into the world of private religion, in which each individual chooses the religious symbol which is most meaningful to him, on the basis of his personal taste.

Becoming a Christian means placing oneself within a community, and recognising one symbol – the cross of Christ – as having been authorised and authenticated by the Christian tradition, from the time of the New Testament onwards. It is this symbol which exercises a normative and decisive influence over the Christian understanding of God and the world, and the Christian cannot choose any other symbol unless he is to compromise the integrity of the Christian tradition. Religious symbols are far too important to be left to the private choice of the individual! Being a Christian means accepting the symbol which the Christian tradition has recognised as normative from the earliest of times to the present day, and which has survived the twin tests of time and experience – the cross of Jesus Christ. Christian faith is a community, and not just a private, matter. The believer does not choose where to look for God, in a decision based upon personal taste, but *is told* where to look, and what shape and form that self-disclosure takes – it is something 'given' to him by the Christian tradition, within which he has come to stand. This point is so important that it needs further discussion.

The cross and the birth of faith

How does the individual come to faith? This question is too often overlooked. Three main means, all closely related, may be identified.

First, *through the reading of scripture*, particularly the New Testament, in which the story of Jesus Christ and his significance for believers is unfolded, along with the demand for faith.

Second, *through being confronted with the Christian proclamation* – what theologians sometimes call the *kerygma*. The *kerygma* is basically a brief summary of the significance of Jesus Christ for the individual, often linked with a demand for faith, underlying much of the New Testament material. The assertion that Jesus 'died for our sins' (1 Corinthians 15:3) is an example of the *kerygma* – it is an interpretation of the significance of the death of Jesus Christ, with an implicit demand for faith. This proclamation or *kerygma* is evident in the New Testament documents, and is encountered throughout Christian history. It consists of both the direct assertion that the crucified and risen Jesus Christ is of decisive significance for human existence and the implicit demand for faith on the part of the individual if he is to appropriate that significance for himself.

Third, *through the worship of the Christian community*, which the new believer must identify with or which he may encounter as an unbeliever and thus be moved to serious reflection. The Christian church has never venerated Jesus as a dead prophet or a helpful teacher from the past (whose teachings would, of course, require extensive modification in the light of contemporary social conditions), but has worshipped him as her risen saviour and Lord. It is because of who the Christian church recognises Jesus Christ to be that his teachings are taken so seriously, rather than the other way round.

These three sources provide a consistent picture of the Christian faith as a response to the self-revelation of God in the crucified and risen Christ. We shall consider these points in some detail in this section.

Scripture, and particularly the New Testament, is not a disinterested account or history of either the people of Israel or of Jesus Christ – it was understood by those who wrote it to be an account of the dealings of God with them, which are concentrated in and focused upon the death and resurrection of Jesus Christ. When we talk about the 'crucifixion and resurrection of Jesus Christ', we are not talking about the bare historical facts of the cross and the empty tomb – we mean these events *and the meaning given to them by their context* in scripture. Scripture testifies to the way in which God acts and the way in which this action was understood and apprehended by Israel and the church – it establishes a way of thinking about God which both *gives meaning to* the crucifixion and resurrection of Jesus and *is supremely expressed in* those events. Scripture witnesses to a pattern of divine activity and human recognition of and response to that activity which is confirmed and extended by the resurrection of the crucified Jesus. Thus scripture provides us with the key to understanding the meaning of the crucifixion and resurrection of Jesus – events which are robbed of their meaning if they are interpreted in terms other than those given by scripture itself. As Luther put it, 'scripture is the manger in which Christ is laid', setting the context for fully understanding the significance of his death and resurrection.

Christ's death and resurrection did not take place in some sort of vacuum, but in the context of a tradition of recognising the redemptive acts of God in human history. In the exodus from Egypt and the death and resurrection of Jesus Christ may be seen the saving acts of one and the same God. The New Testament, from its beginning to its end, exults in the conviction that God acted decisively to redeem mankind in the death and resurrection of Jesus Christ; that this is indeed 'Good News' (and the reader is reminded that this is what the word *gospel* literally means); that it demands a response from us if it is to affect us individually; and that it places certain demands upon us once it has been accepted.

The New Testament is not a disinterested account of Jesus' career, but is a passionate and sustained plea for faith on the part of its reader. 'Jesus did many other signs in the presence of his disciples which aren't recorded in this work, but these are written so that you may believe that Jesus is the Christ, the Son of God, and that believing you may have life in his name' (John 20:30–31). The reader of the New Testament is not being presented with a neutral, balanced and impartial assessment of Jesus Christ, but with the faith of those who recognised in the crucified and risen Christ their saviour and Lord, and the potential saviour and Lord of all those who would follow them in human history. For the New Testament writers the fact that the crucified and risen Christ *is* saviour and Lord is an essential part of his history, and must be passed on to their readers.

The message of the New Testament is 'distilled' in the proclamation or *kerygma*. Much recent New Testament scholarship has identified the proclamation of the crucified Jesus Christ as being risen and charged with significance for the human dilemma as a central unifying feature of the New Testament. The *kerygma* can be regarded as an evaluation of the importance of Jesus, an attempt to identify what is crucially important about him (so that what is peripheral can be recognised as such), and to proclaim the significance of Jesus Christ for those outside the community of faith. To put it very crudely, it is a very compact summary of the response of the church to those outside its bounds who ask, 'What's important about Jesus Christ *for me*?' And that essential summary involves the cross and the resurrection. Just as the preacher or evangelist of today will proclaim that the crucified and risen Christ can, through faith on the part of his hearers, transform the human situation, so the first Christians appear to have done the same.

'Faith comes from what is heard, and what is heard comes by the preaching of Christ' (Romans 10:17). It was through the preaching of the direct and immediate relevance of the crucified and risen Christ to the human situation that faith was generated, was born, in the early church, and through preaching it has been passed down to us. The basis of the proclamation of the church today is the same as it was in the early church – the same cruciform logic, the same appeal for faith in the God who raised Jesus Christ from death upon the cross. To *become* a Christian and to *be* a Christian: both involve standing within a community tradition generated, nourished and sustained by faith in the crucified and risen Christ. The cruciform framework within which the Christian faith is generated and passed down from one generation to another cannot be overlooked or played down by those who wish to suggest that some other aspect of Christianity, more amenable to their private purposes, is its central feature. This is not a matter in which private judgment may be permitted, precisely because of the irreversible 'givenness' of the centrality of the cross to Christian faith and proclamation.

When an individual comes to faith, he joins a community of faith in which he worships God. The centrality of the cross and resurrection to the corporate worship of the Christian church down the ages can neither be denied nor played down. If he is baptised, the sign of the cross will be made upon the believer's forehead and he will be told that he will lead the life of faith in this sign. The sign in which believers go forward to conquer the disbelieving world is that of the cross – it is the symbol and ground of the collective faith of the church, and its individual members, in the God who raised the crucified Jesus Christ from the dead and who is able to sustain believers and the church in the face of the hostility of the world. In that community of faith, believers will worship Jesus Christ as saviour and Lord; they will pray to and worship Jesus Christ *as* God; they will find their attention directed, in the more liturgical churches, to the centrality of the crucifixion and resurrection of Jesus as the central and ineliminable elements of the eucharistic liturgy. In this liturgy the story of Jesus Christ is authoritatively retold, with the emphasis falling upon the crucifixion and resurrection and their importance for believers.

New believers or curious outsiders thus find themselves confronted with a community tradition which shapes its understanding of God and the world in accordance with the cross of Jesus Christ. This is not, of course, to say that this is necessarily the *right* or even the *only* way of understanding God and the world – but it is to say that it is the authentically *Christian* way of doing so. Even before we begin to enquire concerning the truth of the Christian claims, it is necessary to recognise that those claims exist.

A distinction is sometimes made between the *act* and the *content* of faith – the 'faith which believes' and the 'faith which is believed' – as the word 'faith' can bear both meanings. The *act* of faith is the individual's decision to believe, or his attitude of faith, whereas the *content* of faith concerns what is actually believed. Both the *act* of faith and the *content* of faith are brought into being and nourished through direct or indirect encounter with a community tradition which is based upon the proclamation of the resurrection of the crucified Christ. It is this community which proclaims to a disbelieving world the significance of the death and resurrection of Jesus Christ; it is this community which retells the great story of the saving acts of God in history, culminating in the crucifixion and resurrection of Jesus Christ; it is this community whose proclamation down the ages has, directly or indirectly, led to the confrontation of those outside its bounds with the word of salvation in the crucified and risen Christ, and those who respond in faith to this proclamation thus find themselves within that community, sharing its faith.

It will therefore be clear that the faith of the believer of today rests upon the faith of the believers of yesterday, in a process which may be traced back to the first witnesses and heralds of the resurrection itself. It was on account of, and in the light of, the conviction that the crucified and risen Christ was the saviour and Lord of mankind, that the New Testament came into being. Every testimony to the significance of the crucified and risen Christ dating from the lifetime of those who knew him at first hand which we now possess, or ever will possess, is both a consequence of and a witness to this faith. They have been written and preserved from the standpoint of the writer's faith in him. The first Christians knew and worshipped Christ as the crucified and risen one who had won their faith, and they were unable to speak of him outside this context of faith. And, in the course of time, we too have been confronted with and have responded to this proclamation. The faith of those first Christians, centred upon the cross, has been passed down to us. And we are the servants rather than the masters of that faith. It is something over which we have no control, in that it is 'given' to us. It is something which is based upon a pervasive historical community tradition, and the integrity of that tradition is compromised if we alter its content or emphasis. Whatever our personal inclinations may be, we must acknowledge that integrity demands the cross be recognised as the crucial enigma underlying the faith of the Christian church down the ages, the foundation upon which the identity and relevance of the Christian faith stand or fall.

In many respects, the theologian finds himself in a position not dissimilar from that of King Cnut (Canute), who is reputed to have attempted to stop the incoming tide on the English coast. Just as Cnut was impotent against the tide, so the theologian finds himself pitted against the rising tide of the stream of tradition that will either bypass him or submerge him, but which he cannot stop in its tracks. Christianity has shown a remarkable ability to bypass the obstacles which its less responsible theologians have placed in its path.

While the case for recognising the centrality of the cross for personal and communal faith and reflection therefore appears to be overwhelming, this does not mean that it should necessarily assume a similar function within Christian theology. In the following section, we propose to suggest that the cross can, and indeed should, function as the foundation and criterion of Christian theology.

The cross and Christian theology

Modern Christian theology has been oppressed by the spirit of the eighteenth-century Enlightenment, on occasion even giving the impression of being a willing prisoner. Just as many patristic theologians found themselves trapped by the Platonism of their culture, from which they were unable to liberate themselves (if indeed they wished to be liberated), so many modern theologians appear to welcome their imprisonment within the matrix of Enlightenment culture. But the important thing is not to passively accept the dictates of culture, but to challenge them, to expose their provisionality, and perhaps even to change them.

Prior to the dawn of the rationalism of the Enlightenment there was a recognition that Christian theology was a committed academic discipline, concerned with the exploration and clarification of Christian faith. The words of the eleventh-century writer Anselm of Canterbury sum up this attitude: 'I believe, in order that I may understand.' Similarly, Augustine of Hippo had earlier insisted that 'unless you believe, you will never understand'. In other words, faith comes before understanding: authentic Christian theology is about reflecting upon the Christian faith from *inside* the Christian faith itself. The outsider who adopts a neutral and detached attitude to a faith he does not share has no right to be regarded as a *Christian* 'theologian'.

Since the Enlightenment, however, this attitude has changed. A new attitude of mind developed, and it persists in many quarters to this day. For the thinkers of the Enlightenment, it was essential that everything should be justified rationally. What was not rational should not be believed – and one of the greatest obstacles in the face of rational enlightenment was prejudice. It was necessary to adopt a completely impartial and indifferent attitude to everything, in order to evaluate it. Whereas theology had once understood itself to operate within a context of *faith*, the Enlightenment thinkers insisted that it should operate (if it dared!) within a context of absolute objectivity, academic non-commitment and impartiality. In fact, the older attitude to theology was dismissed by the thinkers of the Enlightenment as credulous or superstitious: the 'prejudice' it implied (in that it operated within the context of faith) was quite unacceptable. Anyone who was committed to the truth of Christianity had forfeited his right to be called a 'theologian', precisely because he had already adopted a particular attitude to his subject (in other words, he believed it).

And so the attitude developed that 'theology' was about the rational investigation of religions by those who were completely indifferent to their truth – an attitude which underlies some of the 'religious studies' faculties in modern British and American universities. The theologian came to be seen as a disinterested party, concerned with investigating (from outside its boundaries) the claims of Christianity with complete academic impartiality and indifferent to the outcome of his investigations.

We shall discuss the now-discredited notion of 'scholarly neutrality' in more detail in the following chapter. What it is now necessary to note is the growing revolt against the presuppositions of the Enlightenment that is now obvious in many areas of study and which has considerable importance in relation to our study. Where other academic disciplines have broken free from the baleful influence of the Enlightenment, many Christian theologians appear to be content to remain its prisoner, subject to its oppression. In the present section, we shall note the important contributions made to recent discussion of the nature of understanding by two major recent thinkers, and explore their relevance to theology. This thin summary does not, of course, do justice to the rich material and subtle argumentation to be found in their works, and is merely intended to show the reader who is not yet familiar with these highly influential thinkers the sort of conclusions he will find drawn and defended.

In his major work *Truth and Method*, the German philosopher Hans-Georg Gadamer undertook what is increasingly being recognised as one of the most important

and valuable investigations of the way in which we understand things. The work is a sustained and highly convinc-
ing attack on what Gadamer styles the Enlightenment's
'prejudice against prejudice'.

The strongly negative overtones which are today associated with the term 'prejudice' are a direct result of a
characteristic and fundamental prejudice of the Enlightenment. As Gadamer points out with great force, the
Enlightenment was strongly prejudiced against the power
of tradition to understand the world, and instead
attempted to develop a completely objective method.
Objective truth, it was believed, could destroy the force of
tradition. But, as Gadamer argues, the 'objectivity' in
question was both false and delusory.

Whereas the thinkers of the Enlightenment asserted that,
by breaking free from tradition, one was liberated from
stereotypes of reality and enabled to investigate reality with
complete objectivity, Gadamer shows that this blinded
such thinkers to their own hidden prejudices. A tradition of
some sort is not merely inevitable, but is actually helpful in
interpreting experience and reality. A tradition of accumulated knowledge and insight constitutes the framework
within which human judgment can be correctly applied.
Gadamer emphasises that one of the preconditions of
understanding is 'legitimate prejudice', and argues per-
suasively that this insight is crucial if the Enlightenment
illusion of an absolute reason which creates knowledge *ex
nihilo* is to be avoided.

In his first book, published in 1836, Ralph Waldo
Emerson asked the fundamental question which underlies
the Enlightenment approach to Christianity: 'Why should
we not have a poetry and philosophy of insight and not
tradition?' In many ways, this question lies behind
Emerson's Phi Beta Kappa address of 31 August 1837,
which Oliver Wendell Holmes declared to be an 'intellectual Declaration of Independence'. By breaking free
from tradition, prejudice could be set aside in favour of
objectivity.

For the Enlightenment thinkers, tradition was an

obstacle to the truth, which could be reached by purely rational means without the necessity of involving tradition. Once truth had been attained, tradition may be completely dispensed with. Gadamer, however, succeeds in crystallising the serious misgivings which many had felt concerning this approach. Tradition is basically the development of important insights which help us to reach the truth: Emerson's contrast between 'insight' and 'tradition' (*either* insight *or* tradition, but not both) is misleading, in that *tradition* is basically concerned with *accumulated insights* which are subjected to continual re-examination and re-evaluation both by those within and those outside the tradition. For the thinkers of the Enlightenment, tradition and prejudice could be dispensed with at one and the same time – and yet, as the study of the effects of the Enlightenment 'break' with tradition has shown, all that really happens is that a new tradition arises in place of the old.

In the case of the Christian tradition, we are dealing with the meaning of a historical event – the crucifixion and resurrection of Jesus Christ – to which we no longer have direct access, except by tradition. But, as Gadamer points out, this does not mean that we are denied access to the meaning of that event, as the tradition concerning Jesus is itself the bearer of positive meaning and truth: 'It is not a yawning abyss, but is filled with the continuity of custom and tradition, in the light of which all that is handed down presents itself to us.' In other words, to develop ideas we noted in the previous section, the Christian tradition passes down to us, in the 'continuity of custom and tradition', the interpretation of the significance of Jesus Christ which the first generation of Christians had established, on the basis of evidence available to them (and which is no longer available to us, otherwise we might be in a position to verify their conclusions ourselves), and which had been found to satisfy the double test of time and experience in the intervening period.

No one, particularly the Christian, can entirely extricate himself from the complex tradition to which he belongs, by clearing the ground and starting to build from nothing all over again. For the thinkers of the Enlightenment, to concede this crucial point would be a negative matter, in that it would involve the admission of dependence upon the insights of previous generations, and a contradiction of the principle that all truth must be immediately deducible from universal rational principles. Gadamer's important insights allow us to approach this important insight in a positive way: it is certainly true that Christians cannot extricate themselves from the complex tradition to which they belong – and so they learn to use that tradition positively, as a valid and helpful way of understanding reality.

The believer's exploration into truth does not involve setting out into uncharted territory to explore matters which have never before been encountered – rather, it involves encountering the detailed accounts of others who have made this journey before. They recorded their impressions of what they found, which adequately conveyed their experience to others, and stimulated others to undertake the journey afterwards, shaping their impressions of what they might find. The believer's exploration into truth thus consists not so much in pioneering as in attempting to evaluate a long stream of tradition which expresses the faith to which believer and tradition alike are committed, in order to restate or modify it if the circumstances seem to make it necessary. But the element of commitment to a tradition is an essential part of the theologian's resources, and that theologian is not at liberty to set it aside. Theology is thus something done from within the community of faith, in an attempt to explore and restate something to which the theologian is committed – the tradition.

For Christian theologians in the first millennium, this was exactly what theology was – reflection upon the Christian faith, carried out within the context of faith. In particular, this meant acceptance of certain restrictions upon sources and presuppositions. True knowledge of God, according to the Christian tradition, is found within the Christian faith itself. 'He who doesn't have the church as his mother doesn't have God as his father' (Cyprian of Carthage) – to restate this in Gadamer's terms, it is the

Christian tradition concerning God, mediated in history by the church, which allows us access to mediated insights concerning God. As we have argued constantly in the present work, the Christian tradition is radically cruciform – the cross is so deeply embedded in the Christian way of thinking about and worshipping God that wrestling with its enigmatic form must be an essential component of Christian theology. Anyone who wrestles with the Christian tradition must, in the end, wrestle with the enigma of the cross, mediated by that tradition.

Insights complementary to those of Gadamer have been developed by the natural scientist Michael Polanyi, in his famous work *Personal Knowledge*. In this work, Polanyi demonstrates how seriously misleading the Enlightenment idea of 'objective truth' is, even within the sphere where it might be thought to be most relevant – the natural sciences. For Polanyi, the concept of 'objective knowledge' is only a real possibility if man suddenly takes the place of God, and is able to have access to every conceivable aspect of the universe. But, as Polanyi points out, we have access only to a limited and restricted dimension of the universe, so that although our knowledge is not completely subjective, it lacks the totally 'objective' character which the Enlightenment thinkers believed it possible to attain.

> We must now recognize belief once more as the source of all knowledge. Tacit assent and intellectual passions, the sharing of an idiom and a cultural heritage, affiliation to a like-minded community: such are the impulses which shape our vision of the nature of things on which we rely for our mastery of things. No intelligence, however critical or original, can operate outside such a fiduciary framework.

For Polanyi, a 'fiduciary framework' – a framework of *belief*, of *faith*, of *commitment* – is a necessary precondition of knowledge. Just as Gadamer defended the necessity of 'legitimate prejudice', Polanyi emphasises that a framework of belief is required if knowledge is to come about. The only possible route to knowledge is based upon commitment and an element of risk. This is as true for the natural scientist as it is for the theologian: according to Polanyi, both hold that their knowledge of reality rests upon faith-commitments which cannot be demonstrated, but are tacitly accepted within the communities in which they operate. The scientific community and the Christian church are both 'like-minded communities', to which affiliation by the individual is essential if his understanding of reality is to proceed: understanding takes place within a community tradition. To use Polanyi's famous phrase, science and theology alike affirm the 'fiduciary rootedness of all reality' in the face of the Enlightenment misrepresentation of the situation. This important insight, which is gaining increasing recognition, marks a decisive break with the spirit of the Enlightenment, and underlies Polanyi's personal plea for a 'post-critical' philosophy. Science and theology, so often regarded as mutually incompatible intellectual disciplines, are now increasingly recognised to be converging in their understanding of how we gain knowledge of a reality which can never be totally within our grasp.

It is beyond the scope of this work to discuss the insights of either Polanyi or Gadamer any further: the important point which we wish to emphasise is that there is a growing conviction that the attitude of the Enlightenment towards Christian theology is seriously in error, and that there is an excellent case to be made for Christian theology to recognise this explicitly. Too often, ancient insights are abandoned because they conflict with modern ideas – and, as these ideas are themselves abandoned, we fail to reclaim the insights which were abandoned on their account.

The nature of Christian theology is a case in point: we need to recover the ancient traditional idea of theology as a discipline which arises within the community of faith in an attempt to unfold and analyse the Christian tradition and bring it to bear on the intellectual, moral and spiritual needs of the day. Creative theological scholarship and speculation actually take place within the framework of a specific community tradition, based upon the cross and resurrection of Jesus Christ, which simultaneously *transmits* and *criticises* that tradition, enquiring whether the traditional formulations adequately articulate the truths to which they bear witness. It is thus the theologian who most values tradition who is best placed to criticise it – precisely because he wishes to purify and strengthen it.

The theologian may be in a position from which he may evaluate how effectively the Christian tradition represents, interprets and transmits its basis, the primal event of faith – but neither he, nor indeed anyone else, is in a position to *evaluate* the basis of that tradition, to determine whether it is right or wrong. The statement 'Christianity is wrong' is more accurately stated as 'Christianity is not consistent with my personal view of reality' or 'Christianity is not consistent with the presuppositions of the community to which I belong.' Thus the Enlightenment critic of what we might loosely call 'traditional Christianity' is basically saying little more than 'traditional Christianity is not compatible with the presuppositions of the Enlightenment, which I personally share'. No objective judgment is being made. In the end, the *only* way by which Christianity might be shown to be 'wrong' is by demonstrating that the crucifixion and resurrection never took place – and *this* merely serves to emphasise the cruciality of the cross to the Christian faith.

3 THE CROSS AND THE WISDOM OF THE PRESENT AGE

With increasing regularity, television programmes are produced and books published claiming that most recent scholarship has completely discredited Christianity. Often such works are based upon poor scholarship and present no serious challenge to Christianity at all. But their existence raises a question of considerable importance for this work, and for the future development of Christianity in general: How 'disinterested' is scholarly investigation of Christianity? How much influence ought academic theologians to have over Christian thinking?

For Luther, real Christian theology was based upon a direct and frightening encounter with the living God, in which the believer was made aware of the seriousness and difficulty of the subject: 'living, or rather dying and being damned make a theologian, not understanding, reading or speculating'. For Luther, the best theologian was the true and humble believer. But in order to survive as a subject taught at university level, theology has increasingly had to demonstrate its academic credentials, with potentially serious consequences. How can the foolishness of the cross be reconciled with the wisdom of the universities?

A more serious question concerns the basis of Christian faith itself: for virtually every statement of faith which the Christian believer wishes to make, an academic somewhere may be found who will wish to challenge it. Does this mean that believers must abandon their faith until it has been verified by 'disinterested' academic scholarship? Can they make any statements about their faith without having to submit them to the court of the academic world?

In the present chapter we propose to raise some very difficult, but very important, questions concerning the role of academic theologians and the 'theology of the cross'. Since the last century, there has been a growing revolt against this 'papacy of the professors' (Martin Kähler). In the last chapter, we indicated that there were excellent reasons for suggesting that theology was something most appropriately undertaken within the community of faith, rather than outside it. In the present chapter, we wish to raise certain questions concerning the way in which theology is currently undertaken in academic circles. Though difficult, and at times painful, these questions must be fairly faced, rather than avoided.

How 'disinterested' is academic scholarship?

The traditional view of scholarly activity is that it is a passionately disinterested, if frequently uninteresting, pursuit undertaken by individuals devoid of partisan bias, whose sole concern is with establishing the truth. Like all myths, it is based upon a certain central element of truth. There is unquestionably a deep desire within the breast of many an academic to uncover historical relationships which have hitherto escaped the notice of their colleagues, and to aid the process of understanding the world in which we find ourselves. But this must not blind us to certain aspects of scholarly activity.

The critical work of the Frankfurt School (which was based on the Institute for Social Research affiliated to the University of Frankfurt and was noted for its development of critical theory) has indicated that it is necessary to search for hidden, unstated *interests* on the part of scholars as they undertake their enquiries – undeclared interests that exercise considerable influence over the outcome of their enquiries. We have every right to probe a scholar undertaking an investigation concerning the motivation for that study. Are there any hidden interests we should know about, which might exercise an influence over his interpretation

of the material? Do scholars approach their material pre-
disposed to place a certain interpretation upon it? Some
examples may help bring this point out.

In his major study of the investigation of German history
by scholars in the German Democratic Republic since the
Second World War, *German History in Marxist Perspective*,
Andreas Dorpalen demonstrates with meticulous care the
way in which the Marxist presuppositions of such historians have had a decisive influence upon the outcome of
their historical enquiries. This influence is obvious in two
respects.

First, the Marxist interpretation of history requires that
the peasantry of the medieval period constituted a significant socio-economic force. And so we find intensive investigation of the German peasantry undertaken, not as a
matter of purely scholarly interest, but in order to provide
support for the Marxist understanding of history. Although
Jürgen Kuczynski's forty-volume study of the peasantry is a
valuable piece of historical investigation in many respects,
it is not disinterested or impartial – there is an undeclared
interest on the part of the historian.

The second way in which the influence of hidden interests is evident is the interpretation placed upon events,
which reflects the presuppositions of either the scholar
undertaking the research or whoever is funding or otherwise supporting that scholar. Thus Dorpalen points to
the way in which history is 'rewritten' on account of the
rigidities of the Marxist historical framework.

This is, of course, an obvious case of undeclared interest
on the part of scholarship, and it might reasonably be
pointed out that it is not typical of scholarly investigation in
general. The difference, however, is generally one of
degree, rather than kind. There is a hidden agenda underlying much scholarly research. All scholarly activity is
intended to serve some purpose. It may be the desire to
promote the scholar's career: promotion within academic
circles is, after all, based upon the scholar's published
works and reputation. In investigating a well-worn field of
enquiry, it is often necessary for scholars to develop some

new hypothesis in order to justify publication of their work – after all, the endorsement of an earlier scholar's views is not a promising publishing proposition! It may be the scholar's desire to establish a reputation within a particular group or circle. It may be that the research work being undertaken will be of benefit to the scholar's sponsoring institution or corporation. In all these respects – most of which are tacitly acknowledged within the academic community itself – it is necessary to exercise a certain degree of caution in speaking of 'the disinterestedness of scholarly activity' – disinterested it is certainly *not*: the crucial question is whether the nature and extent of the scholar's hidden and undeclared interests seriously prejudice the outcome of the investigation.

Let us begin to apply some of these insights to the activities of academic theologians.

First, we have to note that academic theologians do not differ from other academic mortals, and are interested in promotion. This hidden interest need hardly be censured, but it must certainly be recognised! Promotion depends upon publications, particularly upon originality. There is little to be gained in this respect by publishing works which simply endorse traditional Christian teachings. Part of the motivation for writing and publishing works which challenge traditional Christian views is generally the scholar's desire to establish a reputation as an original, creative and radical thinker, in an intellectual climate where this is held to be appropriate, and the publisher's desire to sell the resulting book. This is not, of course, to say that works critical of traditional Christianity may be dismissed out of hand as arising from base motives on the part of their writer or publisher. It is simply to recognise, painful though it may be, that such interests *do* exist, and must be taken into account in assessing the 'disinterestedness' of academic scholarship. Western culture measures academic success in terms which are culturally conditioned – the publication of works and advancement in the academic world. This point cannot be ignored. All too often scholars subject Christianity to the most critical of examinations – without themselves, in terms of their presuppositions and motives, being subject to any form of examination. Scholarship reflects – in terms of its concerns, presuppositions and criteria for determining its merit – western culture. As the Frankfurt School has demonstrated, we cannot rest content with asking *what* individual scholars think – we must ask the more radical, more penetrating, and more distressing question: *Why* do they think it?

This point has been emphasised, not necessarily because it is of paramount importance, but because it is all too often overlooked. I myself, currently engaged in a number of scholarly investigations, am as subject to these painful observations as any other scholar. It is necessary to make this point in order to call into question the alleged 'disinterestedness' or 'impartiality' of scholarly assessments or evaluations of Christianity.

There is also a widely held popular view, which academics have failed to disown, that academic scholarship can provide an instant and authoritative pronouncement on the validity of – for example – certain Christian affirmations, such as the resurrection. There is a distressing tendency, particularly on the part of the popular media, to set up Professor Brown from such-and-such a reputable university as the final authority on a question of crucial importance to the Christian faith – for example, whether Jesus really *did* rise from the dead – and to treat his answer as the definitive response on this subject for all time.

Presumably Professor Brown himself knows that the very principles of his subject demand that each and every alleged 'conclusion' must be subjected to remorseless evaluation and criticism within the academic community, and that his conclusions will certainly be challenged, and probably discredited, within a matter of years – yet this point is not made by the media, who prefer to deal with the allegedly 'assured results' of scholarship. The very concept of *provisionality*, so central to scientific advance, is overlooked in an attempt to simplify the questions involved.

The Christian can hardly be expected to alter, let alone abandon, his beliefs in the light of recent arguments which have not yet had the chance to pass or fail the test of time and the verdict of the wider academic community! How many of us have had the experience of comparing, shall we say, scientific textbooks of fifty years ago with those of today, and noticed how the confident assertions of yester-year have been discredited and rendered obsolete? Where the older book confidently stated, 'It is *now known* that . . .', the modern book records, 'It was *once believed* that . . .'

Nor can we overlook the uncomfortable fact that Professor Brown may have certain personal axes to grind, and vendettas to settle, which inevitably colour his standpoint and his assessment of the views of others. The sheer *humanity* of the academic profession is too often overlooked in the quest for allegedly definitive answers to the ultimate questions of life, such as whether Christianity is right or wrong, and similarly the equally great, if not greater, authority of the Christian tradition to speak on this matter is also overlooked.

Let us illustrate this point with reference to the theme which dominates this book: The interpretation of the crucifixion and resurrection of Jesus Christ. It is quite impossible to adopt a neutral attitude to these events. The academic cannot, for example, provide an 'objective' account of the meaning of the crucifixion. For the New Testament, the crucifixion and resurrection are the primal events of faith, and the New Testament itself is written *in* that faith with the object of *evoking* that faith. A 'neutral' or 'uncommitted' scholarly attitude to the New Testament is incapable of interpreting it in its original intention – to evoke faith.

The pretension of neutrality in this matter must not allow us to overlook the fact that this attitude is actually already a decision *against* the faith which the New Testament intends to evoke. Furthermore, the academic will approach the crucifixion and resurrection with the presuppositions of the modern scientific world-view, which differ significantly from those of the first Christians, who operated with a very different world-view, on the basis of which their interpretation of the significance of the cross is based.

As modern New Testament studies have indicated, the

crucifixion and resurrection are 'given' their meaning by the first-century Jewish expectation of the future resurrection of the dead. It is on the basis of this belief that the full significance of Jesus' resurrection (for example, in relation to the kingdom of God and the meaning of history) was realised by the first Christians. The allegedly 'neutral' scholar is obliged to set aside this belief in order to retain academic detachment and non-commitment – and is thus unable to interpret the resurrection in anything like the same way as the first Christians. Such a scholar might therefore be moved to conclude that 'the Christian interpretation of the resurrection is untenable'. A more accurate summary of his findings would be, 'I am unable to share the Christian interpretation of the resurrection.' The same scholar might be prepared to concede that the Christian interpretation of the resurrection is consistent with certain other presuppositions, which he personally does not feel inclined to share – but he is not in a position to *evaluate* the Christian interpretation of the resurrection.

Similar comments apply to the interpretation of the crucifixion. The Christian interpretation of the crucifixion is complex and depends upon a number of presuppositions. For example, Paul's interpretation of the significance of the crucifixion (see Galatians 2:19–21; 3:13) involves the Old Testament idea that anyone who was hanged upon a tree was under the curse of God and as a result was excluded from the covenantal community. Unless the allegedly disinterested scholar *shares* this belief, he will not arrive at the same interpretation of the significance of the crucifixion as Paul. This, it need hardly be added, does not mean that Paul is wrong! It is to point out that it is impossible for the modern scholar to attempt to *evaluate* or *criticise* the New Testament, and hence the Christian, interpretation of the crucifixion and resurrection.

In the present section we have raised some difficult questions concerning the role of the academic and the scholar in relation to interpreting the crucial enigma at the centre of the Christian faith, suggesting that the ultimate interpretation of that enigma must lie within the Christian tradition itself. This, of course, does not mean that the Christian tradition may ignore the established results of, for example, biblical scholarship. It does, however, mean that the Christian tradition is not to be made dependent upon the ephemeral results of modern critical scholarship, but may be liberated from the tyranny of such scholarship through the knowledge that it may only refine, rather than destroy, the basis of the Christian faith. The proper sphere of the interpretation of scripture and its witness to the crucified and risen Christ is within the Christian community of faith, not the academic seminar room. To illustrate some of these points further, we shall consider the rise of the Liberal Protestant understanding of the cross in the nineteenth and early twentieth centuries.

Liberal Protestantism and the cross

We have consistently emphasised the continuity to be found within the Christian tradition concerning the interpretation of the cross and resurrection. While the church has always attempted to domesticate St Paul, whose insights are sometimes a little too radical for comfort, there has always been a genuine recognition within the Christian church that the resurrection of the crucified Jesus marks a decisive turning point in human history, with untold, and perhaps even untellable, significance for the human situation. In the late eighteenth century, however, as the Enlightenment gained an increasingly powerful hold on the minds of western European and American academics, a growing conviction developed that the church had, from the time of Paul onwards, completely misunderstood Jesus. It was not the cross and 'resurrection' which were the centre of the Christian faith, no matter what St Paul and others might have thought, but Jesus' proclamation of the kingdom of God, and the new ethical values which this brought with it. The central feature of the ministry of Jesus, and hence of Christianity itself, was his ethical teaching and his 'religious personality'. 'Liberal Protestantism' is the name generally given to the movement which attempted to reinterpret Christianity in terms which accommodated the rationalism, moralism and naturalism of the Enlightenment-conditioned European and American cultures, and which concerns us in the present section.

For Liberal Protestantism – which became highly influential in both western Europe and America in the late nineteenth and early twentieth centuries – the gospel of the 'Fatherhood of God and the brotherhood of man' was an intellectually acceptable version of the gospel which managed to avoid the difficulties associated with the interpretation of the crucifixion and resurrection of Jesus. Although Jesus might seem just to dispense exactly the same sort of platitudes which everyone already knew from classical philosophy, the Liberal Protestants pointed out that he surpassed the classical philosophers (except Socrates, of course) by dying for his principles. Although it is not exactly clear why Jesus died upon the cross, according to Liberal Protestantism he managed to make an important religious point by doing so. The concepts of self-denial and sacrifice, so essential and beneficial to human civilisation, are perfectly illustrated by Jesus' voluntary death upon the cross, inspiring lesser mortals to do the same. And Jesus was, of course, a mortal, just like everyone else: what was different about Jesus was that he managed to do everything that everybody else was capable of doing, but didn't know about. Thus Jesus' life and death demonstrate what everyone is capable of doing, and inspire them to imitate Jesus' example.

Liberal Protestantism thus represents a reduced version of Christianity, in which the enigma of the cross and resurrection is removed. Jesus' death on the cross is seen as the fitting culmination of his teaching ministry, demonstrating the full force of his personal example and greatness of character. Such concepts as the 'curse of the law' or 'resurrection' were treated as being crude embellishments of an essentially simple tale of a supremely powerful religious personality. The entire Christian tradition, from Paul to the end of the eighteenth century, had seriously misunderstood the significance of Jesus Christ, preferring to concentrate upon the meaning of his crucifixion and resurrection, where it was obvious to Liberal Protestantism that the essential features of the Christian faith lay in his moral and spiritual teaching, in which he demonstrated himself to be remarkably modern, anticipating much of what nineteenth-century bourgeois western European society thought to be good and spiritually valuable. For this reason, Liberal Protestantism concentrated its attention upon the gospels, tending to treat the Pauline epistles as somewhat erratic interpretations of Jesus, obsessed with the cross and resurrection, which they had a mission to correct. In the gospels (except for those sections which made inexplicable reference to such discredited ideas as divine judgment or resurrection) was to be found the new righteousness of the kingdom of God, on which a Christian society might base its ethics. The first eighteen centuries of Christian thought, from the death of Jesus onwards, had completely misunderstood Jesus – by accident rather than design – and it had been the good fortune of university academics to restore to Christianity both its identity and relevance.

The first Christians, of course, knew nothing of such modern ideas as a 'supremely powerful religious personality', and preferred to base their speculation concerning the identity and relevance of both Jesus Christ and (their version of) the Christian faith upon the cross and resurrection. For an understanding of history which declared the resurrection to be an impossibility, they who had witnessed it would have been quite unprepared. The astonishing fact that those who lived nineteen hundred years after Jesus Christ were able to understand him far better than any who shared his first-century Palestinian background and knew him at first hand was put down to new advances in the scientific study of history. In the scheme of divine providence proposed by Liberal Protestantism, the Christian faith was immediately distorted and perverted through the misguided efforts of the first Christians, until the distant day dawned when 'disinterested' European academics should restore to it both its identity and relevance.

The words of a hymn written by a supporter of this theory are illuminating:

> He reigns, the Son of Man,
> All grace divine is his;
> Pierce through the creeds, his features scan,
> And see him as he is.

By 'piercing through the creeds', these scholars believed it was possible to dismantle the dogmatic structure which had been imposed upon the original Jesus and disclose a recognisable and reliable portrait of the real Jesus. It was on the basis of this historical figure of Jesus that Liberal Protestantism believed that Christianity could be reconstructed.

It seems like a dream, and a dream it was. Unwittingly, Liberal Protestantism merely projected on to the distant historical figure of Jesus Christ its own cultural values and preoccupations. Within decades New Testament scholarship had discredited its understanding of the nature of the gospels – an understanding which was in its own day 'modern', but which, like every 'modern' view, is seen as ephemeral in the perspective of history. The theory of the radical break between Jesus and Paul began to lose its lustre in the light of careful and responsible scholarly research. Gradually, the recognition that the cross and resurrection were indeed at the centre of the early Christian gospel, and ought to be at the centre of *any* theology which presumed to call itself 'Christian', began to gain sway. A version of Christianity which had totally eliminated the enigma of the cross was shown up to be a perversion of Christianity – indeed, to the extent that many felt compelled to ask whether it was a version of Christianity at all, since it showed so little contact with the crucifixion-resurrection centred Christian tradition. Was Liberal Protestantism a version of Christianity – or was it actually a new religion, based upon cultural values and concerns, with only the most peripheral of connections with the Christian tradition?

The cross and the aftermath of Liberal Protestantism

The development and subsequent decline of Liberal Protestantism in both western Europe and America is of considerable importance to this study. What, then, did the movement make of the cross? Two points may be noted.

First, the enigma of the cross was eliminated. Whereas the early church had suggested that the cross ought to be the basis by which culture was judged, Liberal Protestantism effectively inverted this order. Culture was the basis by which the cross should be judged – and it was found to be wanting, surrounded by crude ideas of divine judgment and so forth, which the nineteenth century found unacceptable. It is perhaps a tribute to the resilience of the Christian tradition's attachment to the cross that not even Liberal Protestantism was able to eliminate it totally – instead, it found itself obliged to disinvest it of its enigmatic character, turning a risen saviour into a dead martyr. The cross was domesticated and tamed – and robbed of its force.

Second, prevailing intellectual and cultural presuppositions and concerns were elevated to the status of criteria by which both the identity and relevance of Christianity were judged. Whereas the Christian tradition had previously recognised an *internal* criterion for its identity – the crucified and risen Christ – Liberal Protestantism insisted that it recognise an *external* criterion – contemporary intellectual and cultural values – instead. The gospel (and here we assume, for the sake of argument, that Liberal Protestantism may be regarded as an admittedly degenerate form of Christianity) thus came to be trapped in a given cultural situation, without the internal means to extricate itself from it. Through the elimination of the enigmatic internal criterion of its identity – the cross, whose resistance to interpretation, still less reduction, we shall explore further in later chapters – the Christian tradition was robbed of the means by which it could avoid becoming trapped in specific cultural situations. The application of *external* criteria to the theological evaluation of the cross effectively means applying a culturally conditioned ideological criticism alien to the essence of the Christian tradition, which eventually compromises it.

One of the more curious aspects of the Liberal Protestant 'picture of Christ' – its elimination of the enigma of the cross aside – was the belief, inherited from the Enlightenment, that it was possible to understand Jesus better than his contemporaries ever did. The first Christians had seriously misunderstood Jesus, but by an impartial analysis of the New Testament sources, it ought to be possible to re-discover the *real* Jesus. If there was a chasm, rather than a bridge, between the historical figure of Jesus and the crucified and risen Christ of faith, it ought to be possible to cross this chasm and allow the *real* Jesus to enter the modern period.

We can only admire the bravado underlying the assump-tion that it was possible for nineteenth-century professors to know someone better from books than those who lived at the time and knew him at first hand! In other words, the traditional Christian understanding of Jesus could be dis-pensed with, in order to look for, and eventually find, a new Jesus. Although this procedure is now recognised to be a complete impossibility, it was thought at the time to be a real possibility. A simple, down to earth religious teacher and personality was widely believed to be lurking in the background of the New Testament, overshadowed by the idea of a crucified and risen Lord – and if this latter could be eliminated, the real Jesus could be recovered.

What is particularly interesting is not the naivete of the assumptions of Liberal Protestantism – now dismissed by responsible New Testament scholarship as inept – but the 'portraits of Christ' which resulted. For every 'rediscovered Jesus' looks remarkably like the person who rediscovered him! A gallery of 'portraits of Jesus' painted during the period of Liberal Protestantism is a collection of unacknowl-edged self-portraits. As subsequent critics of this move-ment pointed out with relentless force, the 'rediscovered' Jesus was an idealised conglomerate of bourgeois cultural values, reflecting the cultural situation and aspirations of the rediscoverer.

Liberal Protestantism viewed Jesus through the spectacles of the Enlightenment and operated within its 'fiduciary framework' (Polanyi). Its exponents had unconsciously turned their cultural presuppositions into a view of reality which dictated what Jesus *must* have been like – on the basis of which they asserted that *this* was what Jesus was really like, *this* is what the real significance of Jesus was. Perhaps the most famous epitaph to this movement was written by George Tyrrell in the early years of the twentieth century, reflecting upon Adolf von Harnack's views about Jesus (regarded by many as illustrating Liberal Protestantism at its zenith): 'The Christ that Harnack sees, looking back through nineteen centuries of catholic darkness, is only the reflection of a Liberal Protestant face, seen at the bottom of a deep well.'

In its evaluation of Jesus Christ, Liberal Protestantism made a claim to 'objectivity' which allowed it to eliminate the enigma of the cross and break with eighteen centuries of a traditional Christian way of understanding its significance. Those claims to 'objectivity' are now recognised to be absurd – but they were taken seriously at the time. How many more claims to objectivity will we have to endure? Is it not time to realise that *all* judgments concerning the significance of Jesus Christ involve commitment? Is it not time to recognise that all who try to evaluate the significance of the cross do so within a 'fiduciary framework', whether they are prepared to admit it or not?

The Christian tradition explicitly acknowledges that it approaches Jesus Christ and his cross with a 'pre-understanding', within the context of a 'fiduciary framework' – and it ought to be commended for being utterly honest in this matter, where others attempt a pretension of 'objectivity'. The historical continuity of the Christian tradition – for within that tradition, a specific interpretation of the significance of the crucified and risen Christ has been maintained and passed down from one generation to another, from the first generation of Christians to the present day – means that it is the most reliable guide we have to an authoritative interpretation of the meaning of the cross.

The 'pre-commitment' of the Christian tradition, regarded by the thinkers of the Enlightenment (who operated within a different 'fiduciary framework') as an outrage which disqualified that tradition from having any reliable insights into Jesus at all, is now regarded as an integral part of *any* process of understanding. Anselm of Canterbury's words are now taken very seriously indeed: 'I believe, in order that I may understand.' Polanyi might rewrite this, expressing exactly the same sentiment, as follows: 'I operate within a fiduciary framework, in order that I may understand.' The fact that Christianity has traditionally worked within precisely such a framework does not prejudice its claim to possess the *authoritative* understanding of the significance of Jesus Christ, and, as the insights of Polanyi and Gadamer indicate, may even go some substantial way towards reinforcing that claim.

Christian theology is therefore obliged, as a matter of academic integrity, to operate within the constraints placed upon it by the Christian tradition. Theology is indeed 'talk about God' – but *Christian* theology is a manner of understanding and talking about God which lays claim to certain specific insights which ultimately underlie Christian doctrine, ethics, worship and spirituality. To designate a theology, or way of thinking or talking about God, as 'Christian' is not to say that it is right or wrong, or to call into question other such theologies (although this may follow as a matter of course): it is simply to draw attention to the fact that the term 'Christian' carries with it a reference to a comprehensive and pervasive community tradition, extending far and wide in time and space, which academic integrity – to name no other consideration! – demands must be acknowledged and incorporated into our thinking.

The theologian who presumes to call himself or his theology 'Christian' must recognise that he cannot extricate himself from the complex tradition to which he belongs, and set off, as it were, to explore uncharted territory. Rather, he is obliged to recognise that he is presented with a stream of attitudes, 'pre-understandings' and beliefs which have been handed down to him by a long stream of tradition, witnessing to a corporate faith which alone can lay claim to what is 'Christian' and what is not. And, as we have emphasised, that corporate faith is cruciform. The theologian cannot retreat into a world of private religion, establishing his own beliefs, attitudes and pre-understandings, without running the risk of doing what Liberal Protestantism did so impressively: i.e. break with the Christian tradition in order to forge what gives every indication of being a new religion that bears only the most peripheral relationship to Christianity itself – a cultured and bookish religion for cultured and bookish people.

Christian theology and Christian worship

One of the most important recent developments in academic theology has been the increasing recognition of the theological importance of the way in which Christians worship. In the fifth-century church a famous saying arose: 'the way you pray determines the way you believe' (*lex orandi, lex credendi*). In other words, the very fact that Christians worship and pray has a decisive effect upon the way they think about God. Academic theology has tended to treat this insight with a certain degree of scepticism – despite this, however, there is a growing recognition that the way in which Christians worship cannot be isolated from the way in which they think about God. To give one very obvious example: Christians have always worshipped Christ, and prayed to him *as if he were God*. In other words, in their worship and adoration, they treated Jesus as having the status of, or even being identical with, God. There is evidence for this practice within the New Testament itself, and it is even more well-attested subsequently. The obvious point which is being made with increasing force is the following: You cannot expect a believer to operate with one set of beliefs in his study, and another when he is worshipping. The theologian who feels that Jesus is just a good man will (or ought to) find himself embarrassed if he has to worship or pray to Jesus as if he is God.

Perhaps the most celebrated historical instance of this occurrence may be found in the Arian controversy of the fourth century. Arius argued that Jesus could not be described as 'God' in any meaningful sense of the word. He was a creature, like the rest of us – a particularly splendid and supremely pre-eminent creature, to be sure, but a creature none the less. His opponents, such as Athanasius, were able to place Arius in a predicament – from which neither he nor his supporters were ever able to entirely extricate themselves – by pointing to the church's universal practice of worshipping and praying to Christ. According to Arius, this made the entire Christian church throughout its existence guilty of worshipping a creature – which was nothing less than idolatry. God alone should be worshipped, and to God alone should prayers be addressed – and if Christ could not be identified with God, Christians were guilty of idolatry in their worship and prayers. On the basis of such considerations, the views of Arius and his supporters were declared to be inconsistent with Christian faith.

The Arian controversy, and others like it, helped to establish the way in which Christians worshipped as one of the most important elements in shaping the Christian tradition. Even in the New Testament itself, liturgical formulas can be detected; for example, Paul seems to quote these formulas on occasion, probably on the assumption that his readers are already familiar with them (see Philippians 2:6–11, which is usually thought of as one example: another may be found at 1 Timothy 3:16). And, as we have already emphasised, deeply embedded in the way Christians worship is the resurrection of the crucified Christ.

As we saw earlier, the eucharistic liturgy must be regarded as an authoritative retelling of the Christian story, bringing out the centrality of the crucifixion and resurrection to the Christian understanding of God and the world. The eucharistic liturgy (in other words, the communion service) is focused upon the death of Christ upon the cross: the bread symbolises the body of Christ, given for believers; the wine symbolises the blood of Christ, shed for believers. In this worship the relevance of the death of Jesus Christ upon the cross for the believer is emphasised in word and symbol. The solemnity and intense seriousness with which the death of the crucified Christ for his church is proclaimed is modulated only by the sheer joy of the knowledge of his resurrection.

Christian worship is shaped by the cross – and so must Christian *theology* be, unless the theologian is to find himself alienated from the worship of the church. The heart and mind of the church cannot be allowed to go their separate ways, but must be forged together in a cruciform unity. The Christian tradition, stemming from the crucifixion and resurrection through Paul and the New Testament, through the early church, and eventually embracing us, is embodied in specific modes of worship and prayer which establish and preserve its identity and continuity. Likewise, theological reflection which presumes to call itself 'Christian' must be consistent with this worship and prayer, and carried out within this community of faith. This tradition must have a prior claim to represent an authentically *Christian* theology over any other. A *Christian* theology must speak of God and the world at least in terms which are potentially different from those of other theologies. The thoughts of the believer – whether a theologian or not – are, and must remain, centred upon the crucified and risen Christ.

Back to the cross

In the late fifteenth and early sixteenth century, many writers, both humanists and reformers, adopted a programme of reform and renewal based upon the slogan *ad fontes*: Back to the original sources! Irritated by the complexities and seeming irrelevance of much theological and ecclesiastical writing, they argued the case for bypassing these later developments altogether. Rather than wrestle with the intricacies of late medieval thought, it was thought both possible and desirable to ignore them, to bypass them, and proceed directly to the documentary sources of the Christian faith, supremely scripture, and recapture the spiritual experience to which they so eloquently witnessed. Was not the stream of Christian tradition purest at its source? By appealing directly to the sources of the Christian faith, it was believed that it would be possible to experience in the modern period what the first Christians experienced in those heady days of the birth of Christianity. And so scripture was read not as the textbook of Christian theology but as the reflections of those who had encountered the living reality of the risen Christ at first hand, in order that the reader himself might experience precisely the same encounter.

The believer in the modern period may identify with this programme with the greatest of ease. Irritated by the tiresomeness and apparent pointlessness of much academic and ecclesiastical discussion, the modern believer wants to be liberated from such oppression, and be set free to re-experience the faith of the first Christians in his own day and age. If the Christian tradition may be likened to a great river, the modern believer experiences it as a sluggish, ponderous and heavily polluted flow, where he knows that it once spurted forth with a pureness and vitality denied to him in this later day and age. But why should he have to suffer this oppression? Why should he not be able to experience the sheer vitality and exuberance of the first Christians as they exulted in the knowledge that the one who was crucified had been raised from the dead? Why should we not be able to recapture the sheer sense of excitement and wonder which once set the world alight, but now seems trapped in formulas of interest to scholars but not relevant to life? All too often, theologians and churchmen seem to be guardians of the embers of the Christian faith, whereas what is actually needed is someone to fan those embers until they burst into flame once more.

Christian faith is about an encounter with the living God, not about interesting ideas and concepts. And, as we have emphasised throughout this first part of the work, the Christian tradition, from the earliest of times to the present day, has insisted that this encounter takes place through the cross and resurrection of Jesus Christ. The very *continuity* of the Christian tradition on this point allows us to make a daring, radical and exciting step – to suggest that we return directly to its source, to re-experience and recapture its vitality, and bring into the modern age that faith to which every page of the New Testament bears such a vibrant witness. We need to return to the cross and ponder its meaning for us and our situation today, without having to fight our way through centuries of abstruse theological speculation. Placed between us and the cross is a filter which it is necessary to remove – theories, hypotheses, and endless refinements of these, have all been placed in the way of those who wish to return to the source and ground of the Christian faith. The Christian church must learn to return to where she once started from – the tension between the crucifixion and resurrection of Jesus Christ. In the famous words of T. S. Eliot:

> We shall not cease from exploration.
> And the end of all our exploring
> Will be to arrive where we started
> And know the place for the first time.
>
> *Little Gidding*

This book is about returning to the birthplace of the Christian faith, the source of the faith which challenges and nourishes us today, in order to let it speak to us in our situation today. As Luther found before us, it is a refreshing, invigorating and profoundly disturbing undertaking. But it is one which must be undertaken if the Christian church and the Christian faith are not to lose sight of their identity and relevance in the world. And so it is to the direct confrontation of that crucial enigma that we now turn, knowing that by doing so we begin the journey home.

What is the *relevance* of the cross to Christian faith? to the Christian believer? to the Christian church? It is to these questions that we now turn.

Part Two

The relevance of the cross

4 THE INTERPRETATION OF THE CROSS

To return to and rediscover the roots of the Christian faith is to return to the enigma of the resurrection of the one who was crucified. Christian faith had its origins in precisely this enigma – an experience of profound contradictoriness, a riddle which could not be solved in terms of any of the ideas available at the time. And by demonstrating the inadequacy of these ideas, the way was opened for a reconsideration of the way in which God is present and active in his world. How could the glory, the wisdom and the majesty of God be revealed in a condemned and dying man? How could God's chosen Messiah, the one who came to fulfil the law and redeem his people, have been condemned and executed by that people under that law? The fate of Jesus Christ did not make sense. And the enigma was merely deepened, rather than resolved, through the remarkable event which we call 'the resurrection', in which it became obvious that the same man who had been crucified had broken free from the bonds and bounds, not only of death, but also of time and space. What was going on? And what did it mean?

The enigma of the cross

To be a 'theologian of the cross' is to recognise the resistance of the cross to interpretation, and to concede that we will never plumb the full depth of its meaning. We must learn to abandon any pretence to finality in our understanding of its significance, and any suggestion that one generation may dictate to another precisely what the meaning of the cross for them must be. Each and every generation, in whatever situation it may find itself, must learn to return to the cross itself, there to encounter the 'crucified and hidden God' (Luther). In many periods in the history of the Christian church, such insights have been ignored. The great scholastic theological systems of the medieval period have been described as great 'cathedrals of the mind' (Etienne Gilson), an image suggesting stability, organisation and permanence. The theology of the cross, however, is more like a tent pitched by a nomadic tribe as they wander from one situation to another. It adapts itself to the situation in which it finds itself, but is not bound by it – and upon being transferred to another cultural context, it is able to cast off its acquired cultural mantle in order to take root there. As has often been pointed out, the great incarnational verse (John 1:14) is best translated as 'the Word became flesh, and *pitched his tent* among us'.

It is the virtual absence of any necessary cultural component which is one of the greatest strengths of the theology of the cross: it may be preached to Jews or Greeks, and take root in their respective cultures. It can never be trapped by a culture, because of its inner principle of identity and self-criticism, and is able to transcend the many alterations in human culture and self-understanding which have taken place since the 'word of the cross' (1 Corinthians 1:18) was first preached. Christianity recognises no cultural situation as normative, and may adapt to accommodate itself within any cultural situation, in order to transform it from within. Christianity has an inbuilt capacity to adapt and survive – a capacity which her theologians must never be permitted to squander.

Just as the great English and French cathedrals speak to us of another age, which we must now recognise as bygone, so many of the great systems of Christian theology must be recognised as being inadequate for the needs of the present-day church. Their foundations rest in another era and they possess neither the flexibility nor the adaptability which have proved to be the greatest assets of the Christian gospel. In its history the Christian church has continually failed to exploit this asset, placing cultural obstacles in the path of those who feel the strange and haunting call of the crucified Christ in their day and age. The urgent need to identify and eliminate, or at least deliberately minimise, these peripheral cultural accretions to the gospel is one of the most important tasks facing the Christian theologian and apologist today. We shall develop these themes in the remaining chapters. Our attention is first claimed by the tendency among certain modern theologians to retreat from history, to turn their backs upon the concrete historical foundations of the Christian faith, in order to develop a pseudo-philosophical system of faith.

As we have emphasised, the Christian tradition is not primarily concerned with principles, concepts or ideas, but with a historical event – the death and resurrection of Jesus Christ. It was in the aftermath of this event, within its scripture-determined context, that the meaning of the event was unfolded and expressed in terms of such ideas, concepts and principles. Through sustained wrestling with the sheer enigma of the cross, a pattern of understanding the nature of God's presence and activity within his world was discerned which could be extended to embrace the full scope of Christian existence. Nevertheless, the principles and ideas which were developed in an attempt to unfold the meaning of the cross and resurrection must be recognised as subordinate to the event on which they are based. The Christian church has regularly fallen victim to the temptation to domesticate God by reducing him to some set of manageable formulas, or a tame series of principles, however radical. But in the end, we must recognise that God is simply God, and – to put it very crudely – is just too big to fit into any of our neat little schemes of classification. To reduce the meaning of the cross to theological *statements* runs the risk that we will be seduced into at least one, and possibly both, of two serious mistakes.

First, we may detach the theological statement from the event which gave rise to it, and treat it as some sort of axiom from which other statements may be deduced – overlooking the fact that the statement in question is subordinate to the event, rather than an independent or self-evident proposition which, once established, can be analysed. It is, and it will always be, the *event of the cross and resurrection* which requires analysis, and any statements which we may make concerning that event must *point back to it*, rather than *point away from it.* To behave in this way is to assume that the cross is some sort of sophisticated divine educational technique for ensuring that we learn things about God which otherwise would lie beyond us – but which, once learnt, are independent of the means by which they were taught. To give a simple illustration: when I was a child, I learned to count by using an abacus – but once I had learned the rules of addition, multiplication, and so on, I set my abacus aside as a useful, but now totally unnecessary learning aid. Similarly, many theologians treat the crucifixion and resurrection as some sort of theological learning aid, which we may dispense with as we become increasingly sophisticated. There is a perennial tendency to overlook or bypass the crucial question of how we learn our theology.

Second, we may assume that the principles or ideas which we deduce from the event of the cross are not merely self-sufficient, but *definitive* statements of the meaning of that event. This is to overlook the fact that theological statements are provisional interpretations of the meaning of the crucifixion and resurrection of Jesus Christ, which cannot, by their very nature, exhaust the full significance of the event. Human language is inadequate to be capable of conveying the significance of that event *in its totality*, and tends to reduce its meaning to manageable proportions. There is a disquieting tendency among many Anglo-Saxon thinkers to overlook (or, in the name of some primitive rationalism, to *deny*) the sheer *mystery* of the cross. God, even as he has revealed himself in his cross, far surpasses all that we can say or think about him. This is not to say that we are totally at a loss in speaking about him, or to suggest that our theological statements, made on the basis of the cross, are *wrong* – it is merely to recognise that, in the end, they cannot do justice to the all-transcending reality of the living God. Making statements about God is neither impossible nor particularly difficult – the problem only really arises through the misunderstanding of those who think that reality can be expressed in principles or that all truth can be reduced to propositions.

These points are important, but may cause some difficulties for the reader who has not already encountered a discussion of them. In the present chapter, we propose to discuss further the Christian understanding of 'truth', before going on to demonstrate how seriously inadequate perversions of the Christian faith can arise through failing to take the points which we have just raised with sufficient seriousness. In order to bring these points out, we shall look at the principle of the incarnation and the idea that the death of Jesus Christ reveals the love of God to us. But first, we turn to look at the Christian idea of truth.

Truth and the cross

Let us begin our examination of the idea of 'truth' by comparing the ideas of 'being true' and 'being Christian'. For the thinkers of the Enlightenment, these ideas were virtually identical. Anything that Christianity asserted as 'truth' but which couldn't be verified by reason was to be rejected as superstition. The development of this view can be traced as follows.

First, it was argued that the beliefs of Christianity were capable of being defended rationally. Reason was to be seen as an ally in Christian apologetics, and Christian truth could be supported by demonstrating that it was thoroughly rational. Second, it was argued that all that Christianity did was to reduplicate facts which could be known through reason. Third, it was argued that each and every Christian doctrine should be examined in the light of reason to determine whether or not it was acceptable. And so the Enlightenment critique of Christianity began, eventually ending up by producing a rationalist moralism that is better regarded as a completely new religion rather than as a version of Christianity. Jesus was interpreted as a moral teacher and example, with the enigma of the cross eliminated.

One of the basic convictions underlying this approach to Christianity, which persists even to this day, is that 'Christianity' and 'rational truth' are one and the same thing. If you know something by reason, then Christianity can either agree with it (in which case Christianity is unnecessary as it just confirms what you know already) or else it disagrees with it (in which case Christianity is wrong and must be criticised). This very naive approach to the ideas of 'being true' and 'being Christian' has been so influential that it is necessary to look at it in more detail before passing on to anything else.

Let us consider some facts which are unquestionably true:

1   $2 + 2 = 4$
2   The whole is greater than its parts
3   The sun is some ninety-three million miles from the earth.

The obvious question we must ask is this: Are they also Christian? To put the question with its full force: Is the *truth* of a statement sufficient to guarantee that it is authentically and distinctively *Christian*?

It will be obvious that the answer to this question lies in the negative. The first two statements are examples of rational truth – from the definition of '2' and '4', 'whole' and 'part', it will be obvious that their relationship is accurately described by these two statements. They are excellent examples of rational truth. But if they have anything to do with Christianity, the connection is at best remote! The third statement is an example of a truth derived from experience and observation – it is an empirical, rather than a rational, truth. But there will be few who regard it as a characteristically *Christian* truth! In terms of both its content and the manner in which it is derived it has little bearing upon those matters which the Christian tradition suggests are more central. 'Truth' is something to which both the *Annual Review of Statistics* and the Christian faith lay claim – but this does not mean that they can be treated as identical.

Christianity is not concerned with such matters, although it has no reason to dispute them. It is primarily concerned with a particular way of looking at things, with particular insights and emphases. And for the Christian, these insights and emphases are derived from, and justified upon the basis of, the crucified and risen Christ. Truth is not about a proposition being right or wrong – it is about encountering reality and attempting to give as good a description of that reality as is possible. And for the Christian, that reality is disclosed supremely in the crucifixion and resurrection of Jesus Christ. It is quite simply impossible to reduce reality to a series of propositions! This point has been made in relation to the natural sciences with increasing frequency in recent decades (for example, by Polanyi). It is naive to suggest that reality may be totally defined in terms of propositions which are either right or wrong – the crucial question concerns the *adequacy* of our attempts to represent something which lies permanently beyond our total grasp. This is as true of the natural sciences as it is of the attempt to wrestle with God himself.

To illustrate this with an example from modern physics, we may consider the famous problem raised by the so-called 'dual nature of light'. Early in the twentieth century it was realised that two statements about the nature of light were true:

1 Light behaves as a wave
2 Light behaves as a particle.

'Waves' and 'particles' are very different things, and it seemed inconceivable that light should have the properties of both. Although statements 1 and 2 seemed to contradict each other, taken together they represented the reality of the situation. This apparent paradox was eventually more or less resolved through a more refined understanding of the nature of light (the quantum theory), which was developed on the basis of intense theoretical speculation and experimental observation.

With this important scientific analogy in mind, let us demonstrate how inadequate the Enlightenment concept of 'truth' is. Let us ask the question: 'Is light a wave?' – to which the answer is, 'Yes.' The Enlightenment concept of truth thus demands us to conclude that light cannot be a particle, because 'waves' and 'particles' are mutually exclusive. Similarly, if we ask the question: 'Is light a particle?', the answer is again 'Yes' – and once more, the Enlightenment thinker draws the conclusion that, as 'waves' and 'particles' are mutually exclusive entities, light cannot be a wave. And yet the truth is that these statements, though apparently mutually exclusive, are actually *complementary*. The reality in question is so complex that it cannot be defined in terms of simple statements which are 'true' or 'false'. For the Enlightenment thinker, if it is true that light is a wave, then the statement that it is a particle is false – that is the logic of the situation. This demonstrates the inadequacy of the Enlightenment world-view, which treats reality solely in terms of rational propositions! Yet reality cannot be described in this way. As one of the most important quantum theorists (Niels Bohr) put it: 'a complete elucidation of one and the same object may require diverse points of view which defy a unique description'.

Let us illustrate the theological importance of this point by looking at a set of two statements about God, both of which are generally agreed to be true:

1 God is righteous
2 God is merciful.

At first sight these insights are mutually contradictory. The thinkers of the Enlightenment pointed out that God could not be both righteous and merciful at the same time – he was either one or the other, and they argued that God was righteous. Once more their logic is commendable – but their perception of reality is distorted. The Christian tradition has always recognised these insights to be true at one and the same time. Although logical inconsistency may appear to result, this is the result of attempting to express our encounter with reality. As we have emphasised, it is being increasingly recognised that reality is essentially mysterious and is not capable of being summarised in neat consistent propositions. Human thought, when forced to the limits of its ability to wrestle with ultimate questions (such as the nature of God or of reality), seems obliged to use polarities, antinomies and paradoxes. As Alfred North Whitehead remarked: 'Both in science and in logic you have only to develop your argument sufficiently, and sooner or later you are bound to arrive at a contradiction, either internally within the argument, or externally in its reference to fact.'

The Christian tradition has long recognised that it possesses insights into the nature of God which appear on the surface to be contradictory – but at the same time has always affirmed that this contradiction is *only* apparent. To use the appropriate terms, it is noetic rather than ontic – the contradiction arises from the way in which we understand reality, rather than the way in which things really are. The insights gained are complementary, rather than contradictory – in other words, confronted with the fact that two superficially contradictory statements appear to be simultaneously correct, we affirm that they are *both* correct, rather than taking the logically expedient course of denying one to affirm the other.

Some familiar examples may bring this point out:

1 God is immanent and also transcendent
2 Jesus Christ is both God and man
3 Man acts freely under grace.

These illustrate the idea of 'dialectic' or 'tension' or 'polarity', which is characteristic of human attempts to understand many aspects of reality, including both the natural sciences and theology. To fail to recognise this is to follow the method of the Enlightenment – reductionism. Unwilling to concede that our partial grasp of reality involves such polarities, they are eliminated, in order to give a logically coherent but seriously distorted view of reality.

And Christian theology simply cannot afford to compromise its hard-won insights in so naive a manner. 'Truth' is the
precious and hard-won insight into the redeeming presence and activity of God in his world, and the pattern of
existence which it discloses for the believer – a way of
looking at the contradictions of the world.

The cross gives us insights into the nature of God's
character which seem, at least on the face of it, to be
contradictory: God's love is revealed through his wrath; life
comes about through death; and so forth. At the purely
logical level a contradiction seems to be involved – and yet
the Christian is convinced, with good reason, that any
contradiction involved is ultimately due to an innate
human inability to fully comprehend the living God. As St
Augustine remarked, 'if you can understand it, it's not
God' – an attitude which may be contrasted with the
Enlightenment maxim, 'if you can't understand it, it's
wrong'. The cross allows us to encounter the greater reality
of God, and shows up the inadequacy of human language
and concepts to fully articulate that reality.

It is for reasons such as these that the cross has always
maintained a resistance against reductive interpretation.
We cannot distil the meaning of the cross into a simple
single proposition on the basis of which we may deduce
further propositions. As Luther pointed out, 'the wisdom
of the cross is hidden in a deep mystery'. In the end, the
cross, itself mysterious, points to an even greater mystery
which lies behind it – the living God. The mystery of the
cross is not something which waits our question, but something which questions us. Like the interrogation mark at
the end of a sentence, the cross converts a confident assertion into a statement which requires an answer, which
needs verification. The cross continually demands whether
we are confusing ephemeral contemporary assumptions
with the gospel itself, whether we are preaching contemporary cultural values instead of the crucified and risen
Christ.

The evolution of doctrine?

All too often it is uncritically assumed that doctrinal innovations are legitimate precisely because of their novelty. They are treated as the proper outcome of a process of progressive evolution – without due consideration being given to the elementary question of whether this process is *progressive* or *degenerative*. Consolidation and development are indeed the outcome of a forward-pointing process of evolution – but so are degeneration and decay. The passage of time can lead to either alternative – but which?

Perhaps on the basis of an uncritical reading of Darwin's *Origin of Species*, some theologians seem to assume that there are theological parallels to the 'survival of the fittest'. Older doctrines are replaced by more progressive developments upon them, precisely because the inadequacies of those older doctrines have been exposed. The historian of doctrine, however, has to wrestle with a more complicated and intractable situation, which bears little relation to the simplifications of the theological evolutionists – the evolution of doctrine through the continual reappropriation of elements discarded by one generation, but which are recognised to be relevant by another. The Reformation itself is perhaps the most celebrated instance of a more general phenomenon – the evolution of doctrine through the creative appeal to and interpretation of the theology of an earlier age.

Progression or degeneration? Are alterations to Christian doctrine due to, for example, the rationalism of the Enlightenment to be regarded as positive developments or as degeneration? This question cannot be avoided. Neither can the crucial question which follows immediately upon it: On the basis of what criterion is this judgment to be made? What criterion is to be used to determine whether a certain doctrinal development is proper or improper? And it is at this point that the full relevance of the cross as the foundation and criterion of the Christian faith becomes evident. We thus find ourselves turning to face backwards before we can face forwards – looking to the cross for guidance. We are forced to ask whether a doctrinal development is consistent with the cross and resurrection, as we find them interpreted in the New Testament and in Christian worship and experience. The Enlightenment doctrine of Jesus of Nazareth as the moral educator of humanity may be fifteen hundred years more modern than Athanasius' doctrine of Christ as the divine saviour of humanity, but this is not to say that it is a more reliable interpretation of the cross and resurrection for that reason. The seductiveness of the argument from novelty must not prevent us from ensuring that our statements about God, Christ and ourselves are consistent with the foundational documents of the Christian faith, which in turn bear witness to the primal event of faith itself.

The cross and the incarnation

On the basis of the fact that Jesus Christ, having been crucified, was raised again from the dead, the Christian church drew the astonishing conclusion that God had identified himself with the crucified Christ – that Jesus Christ acted as and for God, that Jesus Christ *was* God. It is a remarkable insight, already clearly in the process of being established and explored in the New Testament itself. The cross, viewed in the light of the resurrection, became transformed from a story of pointless carnage and hopelessness to the passionate and powerful proclamation of the God who stooped down from heaven himself in order to bring humanity back to him. Whereas the father of the prodigal son merely waited for that son to return, God himself journeyed into the far country to reach us in our lost situation and bring us home. It is the proclamation of a self-giving God, a caring God, who identifies himself with our predicament in order to transform it.

Anxious lest such crucial insights be lost, the church laid down as axiomatic the assertion that Jesus Christ is 'both God and man' – the idea of the incarnation in its traditional form of expression. It is perhaps one of the most astonishing and important insights of the Christian faith – in encountering Jesus Christ we encounter none other than the living God himself. It is, however, also an insight which can be perverted to the point of destruction. From the central assertion that God became man may be deduced propositions which become increasingly remote and detached from the event which gave rise to this assertion – the cross and resurrection of Jesus Christ. It must never be forgotten that the idea of incarnation is not 'given', but is 'drawn out' – and it is drawn out from reflection on the prime datum of Christian faith, the cross and resurrection.

Let us illustrate this process of perversion with reference to the traditional formula, 'God became man.' Arguing at the purely logical level, it is suggested by many theologians (theologians whom Luther would dismiss contemptuously as 'theologians of glory', who had never bothered to think about the cross) that 'God became man' means 'man is now God'. This conclusion, rigorously applied, destroys the essence of Christian piety. Hampered by a fundamental inability to distinguish man and God, such theologians argue that it is *man* who is the proper object of worship, that it is *man* who has taken the place of God – and this ultimately leads to the view that man has freed himself completely from any necessity to slavishly serve 'a God', because he himself *is* God. This insight is still cherished by some, such as those who value this insight of Nietzsche, as the basis of the final and complete liberation of man – liberation from the tyranny of God. And so man, having freed himself from the 'bondage' of this God, finds himself in servitude to a lesser God of somewhat more questionable character. The rise of the totalitarian state – in Hitler's Germany and Stalin's Russia – and its atrocious consequences shows how little this lesser God is capable of discharging the responsibilities which deification brings with it. The God of Abraham, Isaac and Jacob becomes the God of Auschwitz, Treblinka and Hiroshima.

A second major perversion of the incarnational principle is related to this. According to this version, the principle of the incarnation establishes the essential harmony between God and humanity, so that human history may be viewed as a gradual process of evolution towards deification. The notion of a theological human ascent towards ultimate union with God features prominently in several major philosophical and theological systems, particularly those dependent upon popular versions of the Darwinian theory of evolution. But is this actually what the incarnation is all about?

The simple fact remains that the doctrine of the incarnation does not mean, and was never intended to mean, that the essential distinction between God and humanity, between the divine and the human, has been abolished. It is not a universal principle on the basis of which further deductions may be made; it is the conclusion of intense and sustained reflection within the Christian church upon the mystery of the crucifixion and resurrection of Jesus Christ. In this man, this *unique* historical figure, who alone was crucified and raised from the dead, we are to recognise from the standpoint of faith none other than the living God himself. The full significance of his words and deeds, his fate and destiny, only becomes apparent through the realisation that God has identified himself with this man, so that he speaks as God and for God, and acts as God and for God. This is not a general principle which may be applied to every individual in human history – it is a statement about one person, the one who brings faith into being. The 'principle of the incarnation' cannot be pressed in such a way as to detach it from its basis and thus render it meaningless. The incarnation is a statement about Jesus Christ and his significance *for us*: it is an *indirect*, rather than a *direct*, statement about us.

To treat Christianity primarily as concerning a principle – even one so dignified and profound as that of the incarnation – is to risk reducing the gospel to the assertion of a timeless eternal truth. Christianity is about an event; it is about a person; it is about history. God does not encounter us at the level of principles, but in our historical existence. To suggest that the 'principle of the incarnation' is the essential aspect of the Christian faith is to suggest that the first Christians discovered or invented something within the world of ideas – whereas they actually encountered and responded to a person in human history. We must not be allowed to substitute the idea of the incarnation for the person of Jesus Christ! Wrongly understood, the 'principle of the incarnation' can mark a decisive retreat of the Christian faith from the realm of human history to that of timeless ideas or concepts. Events generate ideas which remain subordinate to those events – that is the essential insight of the 'theology of the cross'. And to those who respond that the incarnation is an event, it must be pointed out that it is nothing of the sort: it is, always has been, and always will remain, an *interpretation* of a particular life, consisting in certain events that culminated in the cross and resurrection. A theology of the cross maintains that the cross remains the unequivocally *historical* event linking Christian faith to worldly reality. And that link must never be allowed to be broken if Christianity is to maintain its identity within and relevance for the world.

It will be obvious that we have no quarrel whatsoever with the doctrine of the incarnation, which continues to represent a legitimate and helpful interpretation of the meaning of the life of Jesus Christ from the standpoint of the cross and resurrection. What we are concerned with is the possibility of a serious misunderstanding of the doctrine, leading to a retreat from the realities of human existence to the realms of speculative philosophy and metaphysics. By insisting upon the logical and theological priority of the cross and resurrection over the doctrine of the incarnation, we are affirming two essential points. First, an event and its meaning are *given together* in history, therefore they cannot be detached from one another. The event is not, so to speak, a container for the meaning, which may be discarded once the latter has been extracted. Second, theory and praxis – interpretation and action – are inseparable. The doctrine of the incarnation represents an interpretation of an event which is itself orientated towards further human action in history rather than intellectual engagement with timeless truths. The doctrine of the incarnation is too important to allow it to be misunderstood –

and the 'theology of the cross' provides the perspective by which its validity and relevance are guaranteed.

The cross and the love of God

The Christian tradition has always regarded the cross as the supreme demonstration of the love of God towards sinners: 'God shows his love for us in that while we were yet sinners Christ died for us' (Romans 5:8). The sheer wonder of this insight has captivated the hearts and minds of Christian writers down the ages. Why should God love us? And why should he demonstrate that love by sending Jesus Christ to die for us? In the words of Richard Crashaw (1612–49):

> Lord, what is man? why should he cost thee
> So deare? what had his ruine lost thee?
> Lord, what is man, that thou hast over-bought
> So much a thing of nought?

The first Christians, reflecting upon the crucifixion in the light of the resurrection, grasped this fundamental insight and preserved it – the insight that God *acted* to demonstrate his overwhelming love for us in the midst of a dark and loveless world. In Christ we have 'met Loves noone in Natures night' (Crashaw). Jesus Christ gave everything which he could conceivably give, to the last breath of his mortal existence, for us – and, as Luther reminded his readers, those two little words 'for us' transform a narrative about somebody else to one which concerns us. It has direct existential significance for us: it is charged with contemporary relevance.

In Christian theology, as in so many other areas of human life, there appears to be a reluctance to talk about issues as they affect us individually and personally – we often prefer to talk about them in more general terms. We are often reluctant to admit that the subject under discussion has immediate relevance for us, perhaps because we are embarrassed to admit that we're interested in it! The

Christian proclamation is not just about the love of God in general – it is about the love of God for each of us, as individuals. Each and every one of us is confronted with the assertion that the same God who created and sustains us and the world loves us with a passion which led to Calvary. It invites a response from us – not from someone else, but from each of us as individuals. Richard Crashaw expressed this point with these words:

> O my *Saviour*, make me see,
> How dearly thou hast paid for mee,
> That *Lost* again my life may prove,
> As then in *Death*, so now in *Love*.

The great gospel proclamation 'God so loved the world that he gave his only Son' (John 3:16) finds its echo in us, as we realise that this great general statement contains within it another, more personal, declaration – 'God so loved *me* that he gave his only Son'. The famous words of Charles Wesley express this recognition:

> Amazing love! how can it be
> That thou, my God, shouldst die for me?

The death of Christ, our God, upon the cross demonstrates the full extent of God's love for and commitment to his world – and, more specifically, us.

The full force of this remarkable insight can be lost by failing to recognise that it is mediated through the cross and resurrection of Jesus. We learn of God's love through the cross, not by any other means. It is not a 'truth of natural theology', an insight which we may gain by looking at the night sky, a glorious sunset or a great work of art. (As we saw earlier, this involves paying highly selective attention to one part of nature or human activity (the more tasteful part), while ignoring pain, suffering and human ruthlessness towards other human beings.) It is an insight mediated through the crucifixion and resurrection of Jesus Christ – and it is not an insight mediated *alone*.

All too often we find Christianity reduced to the bland assertion that 'God is love' – something which is true, but which cannot be considered in isolation. This central insight of the Christian faith is too important to be treated in so superficial a manner – we must ask precisely *what sort* of love we are talking about. The crucial assertion that 'God is love' is mediated through the cross of Christ, along with others (such as the ideas of the wrath of God and the righteousness of God, and the contempt of God for human parodies of divine wisdom) – and while it is quite understandable that some should wish to concentrate their attention upon the Christian understanding of God which they find most palatable and to their taste, they can hardly be allowed to overlook the fact that they distort Christianity by doing so. And this is precisely what has happened in the case of the so-called 'moral' or 'exemplarist' theory of the atonement, to which we shall turn in a moment. But first, one additional point must be made in connection with the present point.

The tender insight that 'God is love' is an insight of revelation. Important though it unquestionably is, it does not exhaust the self-revelation of God in Christ, and must not be treated as if it did so. 'God is love' needs further definition. It is but one piece in a complex jigsaw, a brush-stroke in a painting, which reveals an overall picture of God as he wishes to be known. We must recall the insight of modern quantum physics, so succinctly stated by Niels Bohr: 'a complete elucidation of one and the same object may require diverse points of view which defy a unique description'. In other words, just as a glass prism may resolve a beam of white light into the colours of the rainbow, each of which is essential to the composition of that light, so the theologian must realise that there are many components to the theology of the cross. These components mutually modify and illuminate one another – thus the insight that 'God is righteous' is modified and illuminated through the recognition that 'God is merciful'. And so the fundamental insight that 'God is love' is illuminated by other parts of the same picture, which help us understand what is meant by the word 'love' in this context.

By isolating only that part of this overall picture which happens to be particularly to our taste, we introduce a dangerous element of both subjectivity and cultural conditioning into our concept of God. For we cannot overlook the obvious question: *Why* is it that so many in western Europe and North America identify the insight that 'God is love' as fundamental, where others in Latin America and Asia identify the insight that 'God is *righteous*' or 'God is *just*' as fundamental? The full impact of culture upon the concept of God which we *want* to discover inevitably means, given the richness of the Christian understanding of God, that we isolate and identify one aspect of that understanding of God as normative. In western culture, this has led to the hard-won insight that 'God is love' being construed to mean he is a sugar-coated benevolent God who endorses all the insights of western culture and lends them a spurious sanctity. This concept of God – which owes more to nature-religion than Christianity, and continually threatens to degenerate into sheer sentimentalism – arises largely, if not entirely, through dissociating the insight that 'God is love' from the source of that insight – the cross and resurrection of Jesus Christ. The simple insight that 'God is love' would have cut no ice in the world in which Christianity had to battle for its existence in the crucial years after its birth – and fortunately the first Christians were not seriously encumbered by a culturally-conditioned concept of God which would have deprived their gospel proclamation of its full force.

This point may be developed further. The insight 'God is love' (1 John 4:8) may easily be misunderstood as a timeless eternal truth. But the cross reveals the love of God *as an action*, rather than as an eternal truth or principle. 'God so loved the world that he gave his only Son, that whoever believes in him should not perish but have eternal life' (John 3:16). The love of God is understood to be demonstrated in the *action* of giving, or handing over, his son. God suffers loss through handing over his son to his people, who crucify him under the law. Love expresses itself in acts, and the assertion that 'God is love' is meaningless unless it is attended by actions, just as the statement 'we love God' is meaningless unless accompanied by action on our part (1 John 2:1–6; 4:7–21). In the cross we are confronted with an action of divine love, inviting action as a response. Theory and praxis are held together, where they might so easily be dissociated. If Christianity is to remain a faith of human action, as well as human belief, it must retain its affirmation of the active nature of divine love, and the human love evoked in return.

In recent years considerable interest has been shown in the 'moral' or 'exemplarist' understanding of the cross. The cross demonstrates the love of God for us – and nothing more. Ideas such as the victory of Christ over the powers of evil or death, or the substitutionary nature of Christ's death – which are an integral part of the Christian tradition – are dismissed (both arrogantly and naively) as 'pre-critical'. This strongly reductionist approach to the death of Christ owes its origins to the period of the Enlightenment. The attempts of the apologists of the Enlightenment to find a historical precedent for their views on this matter in the eleventh-century theologian Peter Abelard are now regarded as discredited, and there is a growing realisation that this theory of the atonement, far from representing an authentically Christian approach to the cross, is nothing less than a radical perversion of Christianity.

With the crucial insight that the death of Christ reveals the love of God for us there can be no arguing: but to say that the entire meaning of the cross is contained in this insight, and *this insight alone*, is to employ reductionism where it is clearly out of place. It is one of many insights, perhaps even (by the cultural standards of the west) the most important insight, to be wrested from the cross – but it is not, and cannot be treated as, the *only* such insight. For the thinkers of the Enlightenment, the 'moral' theory of the atonement represented a simple way of eliminating the insights of the Christian tradition (such as the resurrection, the incarnation, and so forth) by arguing that the death of

Jesus Christ represented the supreme example of self-giving, the fitting moral culmination to his career as a moral teacher. Indeed, without this glorious act of self-sacrifice, Jesus Christ would not, for the thinkers of the Enlightenment, have been significantly superior to Socrates, Buddha or Mohammed. The death of Christ served no purpose other than to inspire others to lead a life of self-giving and self-sacrifice, virtues which the Enlightenment culture prized highly. In Jesus Christ we are to recognise a man – a particularly splendid and inspiring man, to be sure – but nothing more than a man. Jesus Christ exhibits all the virtues which everyone else is capable of demonstrating, differing only in the degree to which he demonstrated them.

For the Enlightenment, Jesus differed from others merely in degree, not in kind: he demonstrates what lies within the capacity of everyone and he inspires us to imitate his splendid example. The rationalism, moralism and naturalism of the Enlightenment were all satisfied with this understanding of Jesus, which paved the way for the moral theory of the atonement. Jesus demonstrates that God loves us – and by doing so, discredits unacceptable views of God (for example, that God is angry with us, and wants some sort of satisfaction). The basic human problem is that we have confused, misleading or wrong ideas about God which require correction – and the death of Jesus Christ demonstrates that God is love, and moves us to love God in return.

The thorough reasonableness of the moral theory of the atonement will be obvious. No assumption is made which the rationalist might have difficulty in accepting, and awkward or embarrassing aspects of the history of Jesus (particularly the resurrection, which the Enlightenment regarded strictly as a non-event) were passed over in order to give a thoroughly moral and rational gospel. But the crucial difficulty remained, and still remains for those inclined to adopt such a theory: If Jesus Christ is not God, in some meaningful sense of the word, then it isn't the love *of God* which is demonstrated in the cross. It is what the love of God could conceivably be like, but in that it is not God who died upon the cross, it is simply not the *love of God* which is revealed by the cross. Love, it must be remembered, is something personal, and something which is demonstrated primarily in actions. To speak of God 'loving' us is to speak of God in highly personal terms, and invites us to conceive of God as a person, as an agent. For the Enlightenment, God was essentially a rational or moral principle, ill-suited to such personal language. But most important of all, the idea of 'incarnation' is to be rejected: it is a human being, like any of us, who suffered and died upon the cross.

In fact the Enlightenment theory of the meaning of the cross is this: The death of Jesus upon the cross demonstrates the full extent of the love of one human being for another, and thereby encourages and empowers us all to do exactly the same thing. It is not the love of God which is revealed in the cross – it is human love. God may be left out of the picture with the greatest of ease, and apparently without making much significant difference to the situation.

Perhaps one of the most serious difficulties associated with the moral theory of the atonement is the utter ambiguity of the cross. If the sole insight to be gained from the cross is that God loves us, why should he go about revealing it in so ambiguous a manner? Could not God have revealed this central insight more directly and unambiguously? The Enlightenment felt able to ignore or overlook alternative and considerably more plausible (given their rejection of the idea that God is *directly* involved in the cross) interpretations of the cross – for example, that God is sadistic and enjoys making the righteous suffer; that God doesn't exist at all; that existence is meaningless. In fact it is evident that the Enlightenment merely took one of the many traditional Christian insights into the meaning of the cross – the only one of them, as it happened, with which they could agree – and elevated it into the status of *the* definitive interpretation of the cross. But the church gained this hard-won insight through a process of sustained

reflection on the meaning of the cross and resurrection –
a process which gave rise to other central insights as well
(which the Enlightenment felt able to reject). As we saw
earlier, we must always ask *how* Christian insights are
gained, how Christianity learnt its faith, if we are to avoid
the pitfalls of the arrogant and naive spirit of the Enlightenment. And that involves a return to the cross, to relearn
what the Enlightenment discarded and to rediscover and
appropriate its meaning and power.

Who, then, is the God who discloses himself in the cross
of Jesus Christ? What God are we actually talking about?
The God who lies hidden in the weakness and shame of the
crucifixion is none other than the 'crucified and hidden
God' – to use Luther's highly suggestive and daring phrase.
It is to a consideration of this God that we now turn.

5 THE CRUCIFIED AND HIDDEN GOD

God is revealed and human experience is illuminated through the cross of Jesus Christ. Yet, as the believer contemplates the appalling spectacle of the suffering and dying Christ, he is forced to the recognition that God does not appear to be there at all, and the only human experience to be seen is apparently pointless suffering. If God *is* to be found in the cross of Christ, then he is hidden in its mystery; if human experience *is* illuminated by that cross, then the experiences which are illuminated are those of suffering, abandonment, powerlessness and hopelessness, culminating in death. Either God is not present at all in this situation, or else he is present in a remarkable and paradoxical way. To affirm that God is indeed present in this situation is to close the door to one way of thinking about God and to open the way to another – for the cross marks the end of a particular way of thinking about God. The cross presents us with a choice, and forces us to a decision: To seek God here, in the apparent defeat and abandonment of the cross, or to seek him elsewhere. To take these insights with the full seriousness which they deserve is to begin to think in an authentically *Christian* way about God and the experience of the believer.

In the present chapter, we are concerned with exploring the following question: Who is the God who is revealed in the cross and resurrection of Jesus Christ? The question is of crucial importance; it must not be avoided. The Christian tradition insists that God has revealed himself definitively in the cross and resurrection of Jesus Christ, and that Christian theology is obliged to concern itself with God as he has made himself known. We are not dealing with an abstract concept of 'divinity' or 'eternal reality', but with whoever or whatever lies behind the transformation of Good Friday into Easter Day. Who is this God who is revealed in the suffering and shame of the cross? And what relevance does that suffering have for our own experience of suffering?

Held captive by a picture

In the year 1518 Martin Luther was invited to address members of his religious order at Heidelberg. By then Luther was beginning to be cast in the role of a figure of destiny, and many had gathered to hear the young man speak. In a series of terse statements Luther put into words the thoughts which had preoccupied him since the beginning of the decade: how God might be known, and where he might be found. Perhaps the most terse, and certainly the most important, statement is the following: 'Whoever looks upon the invisible things of God as they are seen in created things does not deserve to be called a theologian – but whoever sees the visible back of God as disclosed in suffering and the cross does deserve to be called a theologian.'

For Luther, we must turn our eyes away from what we would like to look at in creation, and fix them steadfastly upon something repugnant, threatening and puzzling: the suffering and cross of Jesus Christ. There God displays himself publicly and visibly as the humiliated, abandoned, powerless and dying Christ. For Luther, we must abandon any attempt to find God by reasoning our way into the heavenly realms, deducing what God must be like through philosophical speculation; instead we must look at a historical event in which God has revealed himself in human history to all and sundry. The attempt to find God by escaping from the world is shown up in its poverty and inadequacy, through the self-revelation of God *in a worldly event*. All human conceptions of what 'God' must be like are shown up as inadequate and ridiculous, and we are thus humiliated through the failure of our reason and wisdom, and compelled to consider God as he has revealed himself in the crucified and dying Christ. We are forced to set aside our preconceptions of God (which probably owe far more to Plato and Aristotle than to God himself, as we shall see) and concentrate our attention upon the public, historical and visible event in which God has determined to disclose himself. For Luther, God is revealed 'in the humility and shame of the cross', and we must learn to seek and see him there, and ponder on what we find.

Just as God has humbled himself in making himself known 'in the humility and shame of the cross', so we must humble ourselves if we are to encounter him. We must humble ourselves by being prepared to be told where to look to find God, rather than trusting in our own insights and speculative abilities. In effect we are forced to turn our eyes from contemplation of where we would like to see God revealed, and to turn them instead upon a place which is not of our own choosing, but which is given to us. As the history of human thought demonstrates, we like to find God in the beauty of nature, in the brilliance of an inspired human work of art or in the depths of our own being – and instead, we must recognise that the sole *authorised* symbol of the Christian faith is a scene of dereliction and carnage. We are held captive by the picture of the dying Christ. Precisely because God overthrows speculative theology by making himself a historical and worldly reality, we are forced, against our wishes, to rethink, perhaps even abandon, our hard-won philosophical insights, in order to come to terms with God's revelation of himself as he would have us know him, in the crucified Jesus. God becomes an iconoclast, shattering our neat conceptual pictures of what he must be like by revealing himself in a way which both contradicts and mocks our attempts to pin him down. The cross reveals the fundamental uncontrollability of God, who breaks the mould of our thinking. We are forced, to use Luther's words, 'to begin all over again'. The God with whom we are dealing, the God who addresses us in the cross is – to use

Luther's breathtakingly daring phrase – 'the crucified and hidden God'.

The hidden revelation of God

God is revealed in the cross – but he doesn't seem to be there. The terrible cry of dereliction, 'My God, my God, why have you abandoned me?', brings home to us the apparent God-forsakenness of the cross. It is here that Luther's phrase 'the visible back of God' is so important. Luther appeals to the experience of Moses at Sinai, in which God declares to Moses: 'you shall see my back – but my face you will never see' (Exodus 33:23). Moses is denied a vision of the face of God – a revelation of God *recognisable as God* – and instead is granted a *real, but not necessarily recognisable*, revelation of God. Although it is indeed none other than God himself who is revealed in the 'sufferings and cross of Christ', he is not recognisable as God *on account of our presuppositions of what God ought to be like, and what form his revelation ought to take.* We expect a revelation of the 'face of God' in his creation, and are either unable to find it or else make an idol of what we do find.

For Luther, creation reveals a provisional notion of God, inadequate as an understanding of what God is like, but adequate to serve as a 'point of contact'. God addresses himself to this provisional idea of himself, in order simultaneously to build upon it and destroy it. Addressing itself to the concepts of 'God' which we have formed or been given, the cross breaks them down, in order that 'true theology and the knowledge of God' may take their place. The authentically *Christian* understanding of the nature of God arises amidst the ruins of our efforts to master and control him. From the wreckage of our attempts to pin God down in the manner of a textbook comes the realisation that God is simply God, and we must respond to him as he has made himself known, rather than attempt to dictate to him what he *ought* to be like, or the manner in which he *ought* to make himself known. Theology and Christian faith are about encountering and experiencing the living God, which involves setting aside prior ideas about his nature – and it is through the cross that this definitive encounter takes place.

The cross is, of course, given its meaning through the resurrection. It is in the light of the triumph of Easter Day that the debacle of Good Friday is to be seen. The resurrection both establishes and demonstrates God's overturning of the dereliction of the cross, disclosing the hidden presence of God in that situation. We must avoid thinking that the cross represented a scene of *apparent* weakness, concealing the divine strength, a theological wolf in sheep's clothing. Instead, the strength of the resurrection was demonstrated *through* the real weakness of the crucified Christ, demonstrating the transformational power of the divine activity, rather than the mere stripping away of the disguise of weakness and mortality. Christ went to the cross *for us*, as one of us, sharing our mortality and frailty. The weakness, hopelessness, sufferings and death which he experienced are those which *we* experience. Christ passed through this hell of suffering and consecrated it to God, thereby lending dignity to the darkest aspects of the human predicament.

The resurrection forced the first Christians to the realisation that the one who they had thought was cursed by God had been raised by him to glory. The mission which they had thought was ended by the cross was shown only to have begun. The great themes of vindication, restoration, transformation and exaltation compete with each other as the New Testament writers attempt to put into words the incredible conclusions which followed from an unthinkable change in the situation. What they had thought was the end of a book proved merely to be its preface. 'Blessed be the God and Father of our Lord Jesus Christ! By his great mercy we have been born anew to a living hope through the resurrection of Jesus Christ from the dead' (1 Peter 1:3 RSV). The cross was seen in a new light, and given a new meaning, being transformed from a symbol of death and despair to a symbol of new life and hope. The great

Christian themes of 'life-through-death' and 'recovery-through-loss' derive from the overturning of a situation which was initially thought to mean nothing but death and loss.

Why then identify the cross as the point at which God addresses us and reveals himself? Why not single out the resurrection as disclosing the nature and purposes of God, given its evident importance to the interpretation of the crucifixion? With this question, we come to a central feature of our study. The Christian faith is addressed to us as we exist here and now, as we struggle to make sense of our own situation and our ultimate destiny. It illuminates and transforms our present situation by pointing to the pattern of crucifixion and resurrection disclosed in the destiny of Jesus Christ, and apprehended and appropriated by faith on the part of the individual believer. Through faith we are assured that the destiny of the one who was crucified and raised is *our* destiny – we learn to read *our* personal history into the story of the cross. The cross is the mirror which reflects the paradoxes of the Christian life. '[We are] fellow heirs with Christ, provided we suffer with him in order that we may also be glorified with him. I consider that the sufferings of this present time are not worth comparing with the glory that is to be revealed to us' (Romans 8:17–18 RSV).

The believer's quest for meaning takes place here and now, not in the heavenly realms. It is a symbol which speaks directly to the present human situation, rather than its future transformation, which is required. We need reassurance that God really is present *here and now*, in the contradictions and confusions of human experience. Where is God, in a world of meaninglessness, suffering and death? God may be in heaven – *but is he here?* And it is for reasons such as these that the Christian tradition, following in the paths indicated by Paul, has identified the cross, *interpreted in the light of the resurrection*, as the final, decisive and normative locus of the revelation of God. It, and it alone, must be the basis and foundation of the Christian understanding of existence. It, and it alone, must be the criterion by which the church judges its doctrine and its actions, its beliefs and its deeds. It, and it alone, must function as the basis of the proclamation of Christ to a world which believes him to be absent, which believes that it has forced God out of it. In all these matters, we must learn to cling fast to the 'crucified and hidden God' who was present in the 'sufferings and the cross of Jesus Christ' – for he whom we otherwise could not grasp has given himself to us.

Life under the cross involves living Good Friday in the light of Easter Day, knowing that God is neither absent from nor uninvolved in the former, but is present and working in a strange and hidden way – a way which can only be fully disclosed when time gives way to eternity, but which is illuminated by the resurrection. There is a dialectic, a tension, between the cross and the resurrection in Christian experience.

The contradictions, confusions and doubt which are so prominent a feature of Good Friday are resolved through the astonishing events of Easter Day – but the fact remains that it is these contradictions, confusions and doubts which characterise much of our experience as Christians in the world. We have to recognise the resurrection as being 'not yet', and yet at the same time 'already present' – the 'there and then' which breaks into the 'here and now' and casts light upon the present situation without altering it *except in that we are allowed to view that situation in a new light*. It is therefore important to know that the sheer enigma of Christian existence in a world from which God seems forced out is already *disclosed* in the crucifixion, and already *resolved* in the resurrection.

The perplexing and contradictory character of Christian existence is no novelty, discovered by believers in the present century, but is a perpetual feature of the Christian life down the ages. Although the full weight of this question may be blunted by social or cultural circumstances in many situations, it particularly forces itself on individuals and a perhaps too unwilling church at moments of crisis, when their identity, relevance and continued existence are at stake.

The crucified God

Where is God to be found? By answering, 'The cross alone is our theology,' we are effectively saying that the cross has the final word to say about God. The characteristically *Christian* concept of God is disclosed in the cross. We shall explore these insights later, particularly in relation to the problem of suffering and evil. For the moment, however, our attention is claimed by a question of no less importance: How can we talk about God in a world in which the word 'God' has lost much of its meaning? How are we *authorised* to use this word 'God'?

Before beginning to answer this question, we must point out that many recent North American and western European writers have been seduced by the suggestion that God 'died' in their cultures quite recently. In other words, there is a widespread supposition in certain circles that to speak of 'God' in North America or western Europe is to use a word which has been rendered meaningless, or a concept which was exposed as devoid of all relevance, by cultural developments from the dawn of the Enlightenment onwards.

There is unquestionably some truth in the suggestion that a significant shift in attitudes towards both the word and the concept of 'God' took place in some sections of North American and western European society at this point. It would, however, be foolish to extrapolate from this observation to other cultures (in the two-thirds world, for example, where 'God' gives no indications of cultural rigor mortis), or even to suggest that this represents a *permanent and developing* shift in the cultural situation, so that Christianity will effectively be unable to communicate its ideas in the years which lie ahead. Cultural situations change, and the perceived relevance of such concepts as 'God' changes with them – and if the Christian church permits *external* considerations to determine the perceived relevance of its proclamation and continued existence, it will find itself trapped in a cultural spiral, as it continually attempts to adjust its proclamation in the wake of cultural changes. (We use the phrase 'in the wake of' deliberately, based on the observation that most Christian churches take several decades to respond to such shifts, by which time those original shifts have themselves given way to new developments, thereby blunting the force of that response somewhat.)

If Christianity is to address itself to, rather than merely attempt a derivative response to, contemporary society, it must regain the fundamental insight that it possesses now, as it always has, an *internal* criterion by which it may judge both its identity and its relevance. The gospel proclamation of the direct relevance of the resurrection of the crucified Christ is the most *God-given* aspect of the Christian faith – and, to put it very crudely, if it ceases to be 'relevant', it is God's fault for making this the central element of the gospel proclamation. Behind the apparently unsophisticated and 'irrelevant' gospel proclamation must be seen the power of God, which has sustained the Christian church and the Christian faith in times of doubt and anxiety. Perhaps there is a need to regain our confidence in the gospel, in that we seem to have lost our nerve to trust it as something which is God-given, rather than the product of inventive human minds. 'I decided to know nothing among you except Jesus Christ and him crucified . . . that your faith might not rest in the wisdom of men but in the power of God' (1 Corinthians 2:2–5 RSV).

In spite of everything, then, we go on saying 'God'. But what do we mean by the word? What do we expect our hearers to think of when we mention this word? With this question, we begin to move towards appropriating the full power and relevance of the cross to the Christian proclamation. Let us consider two quite distinct, although related, questions, both of which are familiar to anyone who has attempted to explain or defend his faith to someone who does not share it:

1 How can I find God, when I only experience his absence?

2 How can I believe in God in a world of pain and suffering?

The first question deals with the knowledge of God in a cultural situation from which he has been forced out, and in which the word 'God' must be learnt anew. The second deals with the problem of *theodicy* – the relation of God to pain and suffering. Although the force of events such as the First and Second World Wars, and particularly the horrors of Auschwitz and Hiroshima, are gradually being eliminated from western European and North American consciousness, they are still remembered with sufficient intensity to prevent the question of God's relationship to such suffering from being overlooked. In the following two sections we shall consider each of these questions, and indicate how the 'theology of the cross' begins to answer them.

Learning 'God' all over again

According to Dietrich Bonhoeffer, modern society lives *etsi Deus non daretur*, 'as if God didn't exist'. As a global judgment, this is clearly far from true – but it certainly *is* true in relation to certain groups in modern western culture. For many, life is lived without reference to God, and the very word 'God' is reduced to a code or cipher without any point of contact with human experience. Although many of the judgments made in the 1960s concerning the irreversible development towards a future 'religionless society' now seem quite unrealistic, there still remain many for whom the word 'God' has no meaning. It must be learnt all over again.

The traditional weapons of Christian apologetic are of little use in these circumstances. The arguments for the existence of God, never particularly persuasive at the best of times, cut no ice here – precisely because they are concerned with the *idea* of God (or something which purports to be a God, until closer inspection reveals otherwise). The question at issue concerns not the *idea* but the *reality* of God. The idea of God will unquestionably continue in circulation without any difficulty, even if it may eventually only be found in textbooks of the history of thought unless the Christian church takes its responsibilities in this area with full seriousness. But the pressing question concerns the reality of God: How can God be proclaimed in and to a world from which he has been pushed out?

With this point in mind, we turn to the cross. To those watching the death of Jesus Christ, God must have seemed to have been pushed out of the situation. There was no *Deus ex machina* to swoop down from heaven, free and revive the dying man, and create a sensation among those who watched and waited for exactly such a possibility. The dreadful cry from the cross, 'My God, my God, why have you forsaken me?', speaks poignantly of a situation in which God was absent, or at least not perceived to be present. The crisis of faith which we all too easily think is a modern invention, felt only by those in the modern period, was born at Calvary, if not before. The moment of Christ's death marked the end of an era of understanding the way in which God operates: those who waited for transformation by intervention could only conclude that God was impotent or non-existent.

This is not, of course, to deny that a real experience of God is within our grasp. For most Christians, there are moments when the experience of God's presence is felt so strongly that they can speak of being caught up in a 'transport of delight'. The believer's exultation in the presence of God is a normal, and thoroughly healthy, aspect of Christian experience. But there are moments, perhaps long periods, when God is absent, when all seems dark, rather than light. And in these moments we are brought back to another moment in history when all seemed dark, when God seemed absent. We are reminded of the strange and apparently contradictory way in which God is present and active in his world, for which the enigma of the cross serves as our most reliable guide. There is a sense in which all our thinking about God, all our attempts to make sense of faith in the world, is illusory – precisely because it is inadequate to encapsulate the living God.

In the moments in which we are conscious of God's absence we are being invited to direct our thoughts to another moment in history when God seemed conspicuously absent. It is perhaps worth recalling that Christianity has its roots in a moment of supreme darkness, as Christ hung dying at Calvary. The transformation of that darkness into light, as Good Friday gave way to Easter Day, constitutes the basis of the Christian hope – that the dark night of faith will finally give way to the dawn of the resurrection life. But in the meantime we struggle on in the twilight world of faith, taking comfort from the knowledge that 'salvation is nearer to us now than when we first believed; the night is far gone, the day is at hand' (Romans 13:11–12 RSV). The cross remains the present reality, with the resurrection as the future hope – a hope which breaks into the present, transforming our understanding of the situation, but not the situation itself. It is the 'there and then' which illuminates the 'here and now', but which remains 'there and then'.

Paul develops this tension between the 'now' of the cross and the 'then' of the resurrection in 1 Corinthians – a letter which, as we have already noted, appears to be directed against those who suggested that the age to come had already been consummated. To those who argued that 'the prize was already won', Paul replied that the present was a time of struggle and conflict leading up to the ultimate goal of victory (1 Corinthians 9:24–27). The claim to victory and consummation of salvation here and now is treated by Paul as premature: the present is, and must remain, a time of struggle and uncertainty, dominated by the hope of the divine transformation of the situation. Paul's understanding of the tension between the 'already' and the 'not yet' is particularly evident in his discussion of the eucharistic celebration. 'For as often as you eat this bread and drink the cup, you proclaim the Lord's death until he comes' (1 Corinthians 11:26 RSV). The present is interpreted in the light of a confident expectation of the future – but a future which remains 'there and then'. It is this tension which dominates and characterises Christian existence. If we think we can eliminate it, we have failed to understand the roots of our faith.

It is this understanding of the absence of God which provides a basis for the Christian proclamation in the secular, godless world. To those who declare that they cannot conceive of God, we invite them to stop trying to do so, and instead contemplate the cross. The cross is a concrete, tangible historical event, easily visualised through a thousand portraits and countless icons. It is a scene from human history which can be described, not an idea which can only be plucked out of thin air. And as the narrative takes in the despair and despondency of the situation, culminating in the death of Jesus Christ, the feeling that God is not there can be addressed directly – before the narrative changes its pitch and tenor, as the events of Easter Day are unfolded, the joy of the disciples described, and the astonishing expansion of the gospel documented. And the crucial question to be asked is this: What was going on? 'God', the word which is to be relearnt, is the unseen actor in this drama of death turned to life, night turned to day, despair turned to joy and loss turned to recovery. The crucial question now being asked is not 'Do you believe in God?', or 'Can you conceive of God?' – it is a question about a historical event: 'What do *you* think happened?'

By doing this we are directing attention away from questions of metaphysics and cultural consciousness of God and are forcing discussion of the root and ground of the Christian faith, the primal event of the faith of the first Christians, and potentially the ground of the same faith today. What actually happened? And how are we to account for what happened? The answers given, and further answers given in response, will parallel those given throughout the period of Christian existence, beginning even in the aftermath of the cross itself – but the discussion is grounded in an *event*, in a *worldly situation*, and not in the somewhat rarefied atmosphere of metaphysical speculation. Our proclamation of God is brought down to earth, where it should always have been. To those who need to relearn the word 'God', we may give a provisional working definition, on the basis of which further insights may be gained: 'God' is whoever or whatever turned Good Friday into Easter Day.

The resurrection of the crucified Jesus Christ allows us to begin to think of God in terms of the one who raised Jesus Christ from the dead, who so dramatically altered the situation of the crucifixion, and with it our perspective of both the cross and our own situation. It forces us to reconsider, in terms of his vindication and exaltation, both the person and the preaching of Jesus Christ. We come to consider his person and message from the perspective of the resurrection, knowing that whoever or whatever raised him from the dead – whether person or power – is intimately linked with them both. The same power or person who raised the crucified Jesus Christ is made available, or makes himself available, through the gospel, to be appropriated by faith. The empty cross, as much as the empty tomb, speaks eloquently of the power of God made available in and through weakness.

This point is important, not merely because of its apologetic relevance, but also because of an underlying theological affirmation. In the enigma of the cross God may be discerned within human history, within the world. God clothed himself with the garment of the world in order that those who are tempted to be seduced by speculation and those who find such speculation pointless might learn to find him in a historical event *in the world*. 'That which was from the beginning, which we have heard, which we have seen with our eyes, which we have looked upon and touched with our hands . . .' (1 John 1:1 RSV). The sheer astonishment of the writer as he unfolds his story of God made tangible in a historical event, can hardly be overlooked. Those who presuppose that there is nothing more to reality than what they encounter in the world are not excluded from coming to faith in God – precisely because God encounters us through a worldly event which we can picture, which we can re-enact and which acts as a starting point for the crucial question which it raises: Who or what stands behind this astonishing event?

The cross is the point of contact between the Christian

faith and the secular world – a task to which it is far better suited than the cultural compromises and existentialist reductions through which Christian apologists have attempted to mediate a reduced version of the faith to those outside its bounds. The cross is, so to speak, the *authorised* vehicle of Christian apologetics, simultaneously providing a point of contact with unbelief while maintaining the authentic identity of Christian faith without compromising it in a misguided attempt to 'make it more acceptable to the world'. It is through the proclamation of the cross that God finds his way back into a world from which he has been excluded.

The God who is hidden in suffering

In the course of its expansion into the Mediterranean world, the Christian faith encountered, and found itself in conflict with, alternative understandings of the nature of God. One such understanding of the nature of God was that he was utterly remote from this world and uninvolved in it. This God was beyond suffering and pain, so that he was not involved in this crucial aspect of human existence. This concept – sometimes referred to as the divine *apatheia* – began to influence Christian thinking, until it was eventually incorporated into the classic medieval understanding of the nature of God, as presented by Thomas Aquinas. The present century, with its experience of human violence and suffering on a hitherto unimagined scale, has seen a strong emotional reaction against this concept of God, particularly expressed in what is known as 'protest atheism'.

Perhaps the most famous, and certainly the most often quoted, example of this 'protest atheism' is to be found in Dostoevsky's novel *The Brothers Karamazov*. Written in the nineteenth century, the story is told of a servant boy who throws a stone which accidentally injures the paw of a general's dog. The general then forces the boy to run naked in front of a pack of hounds, who tear him to pieces in front of his mother's eyes. After Ivan Karamazov narrates this story to his brother, Alyosha, he explains how he cannot accept that such a world is *God's* world: 'It's not God that I don't accept, Alyosha, only I most respectfully return him the ticket.' Similar views have been expressed, particularly in western Europe since the Second World War. For many Jewish writers in particular, the suffering of the Jewish people in Auschwitz has forced them to the conclusion that atheism is the only legitimate response to such a situation.

And so God is rejected because of the evil and suffering in the world. But does suffering and pain cease as a result? Do humans suddenly stop doing evil things? Are those states committed to atheism notable for their elimination of human misery and pain or their respect for human rights? The human predicament remains the same: God may be abolished – but evil and suffering remain. Having abolished God, who can now be held responsible for evil? Having allegedly liberated himself from one god, humanity now finds itself enslaved to another lesser god, incapable of discharging those responsibilities which divinity might be thought to involve – himself. All too often the critics of God would have us believe that his abolition from our world of ideas would simultaneously lead to the abolition of evil and suffering from the world of reality – but it is obvious that nothing of the sort happens.

The espousal of atheism has done nothing to abate human suffering. Suffering remains an unexplained and undefeated reality which atheism can neither explain nor eliminate. Despite all social and political engineering, the total elimination of human pain and suffering remains a utopian illusion, a dream which only accentuates, rather than diminishes, the harshness of the human situation. Ivan Karamazov may hand God back his ticket – but the journey through pain and suffering to an unknown destination continues, despite the hopeless gesture of defiance. Karamazov cannot just stop the world and get off, as if life were a pleasure trip which had failed to live up to his expectations or his taste. Life goes on, defying all our protests.

No ideology – whether it is some form of atheism or

revolutionary Marxism – has unravelled the enigma of evil, still less eliminated it. It remains a grim feature of reality which all the protest atheism in the world has failed to eliminate. Worse still, it loses any meaning. In the darkness of evil and suffering the gospel offers a glimmer of light where there is otherwise nothing but darkness – that God is with us and alongside us, sharing our suffering and pain. One of the most powerful insights Christianity has bestowed to the world is that, in his tender mercy, God entered into human suffering and breathed into it the fragrance of divinity. God has been there before us. The loss of this insight is tantamount to an assertion that a central and ineliminable element of human existence is meaningless and pointless, a constant question mark placed against the meaning of human existence. Those who would abolish God on account of suffering unwittingly empty that suffering of any dignity and meaning.

The view that the existence of suffering and evil either permits or causes us to cease to believe in God must be recognised to be a thoroughly modern idea. Christian thinkers before the Enlightenment were perfectly aware of the problems raised by the existence of evil. The writings of Irenaeus and Augustine from the patristic era, of Thomas Aquinas from the medieval period, and Luther from the Reformation period, are an eloquent and adequate testimony to this fact. But the same difficulties which the Enlightenment thinkers regarded as grounds for disbelief are treated by Luther and others as a stimulus for further reflection, an incentive to deeper reflection on the nature and purposes of God, particularly as disclosed in the death and resurrection of Jesus Christ. Why should this be the case? The facts have not changed: nature remains 'red in tooth and claw' (Tennyson), and humanity retains its tendency towards violence and cruelty which may at best be repressed but not eliminated. What has changed is the interpretation placed upon these facts. It is almost as if the Enlightenment was searching for a 'natural anti-theology' to justify its abandonment of the traditional Christian framework. However, the facts in themselves demand no such conclusion, but merely a closer examination of both our understanding of the nature of God and the sources upon which that understanding is based. The 'theology of the cross' is an alternative interpretation of those same events which the Enlightenment regarded as the basis of atheism.

Why should such suffering and pain cause us to turn against God? Since the time of the eighteenth-century philosopher David Hume it has been widely recognised that arguments about the 'best possible world' are somewhat pointless. This *is* the world as we know it, and the human situation is characterised by a certain degree of pain and suffering. It is as meaningless to say that a world could have been created in which suffering and pain could be eliminated as it is to suggest that a world could have been created in which pain and suffering are even more pervasive and arbitrary than we now know them. No amount of tinkering around with ideas is going to eliminate the grim reality of evil. And to blame God for Hiroshima or Auschwitz, as some of the more bizarre and less responsible participants in this debate appear to do, as if there were no human actors in the tragedies, is about as realistic as blaming the entire Jewish people for the death of Jesus Christ. The first casualty in any such highly emotive discussion of God and suffering is usually a sense of realism. Hiroshima and Auschwitz alike were human tragedies, perpetrated by human beings against their fellow human beings – and to pretend that it's all God's fault is perhaps the least effective way of ensuring that they never happen again. The bomb that shattered Hiroshima did indeed unmask an illusion – the secular utopian belief in inevitable progress, based upon the related belief in the controllability of the historical process. But the illusion that God intervenes in each and every crisis to avert pain, suffering and death had been shattered long before – at Calvary. '[God] did not spare his own Son, but gave him up for us all' (Romans 8:32 RSV). The full meaning of the name given to Jesus – *Emmanuel*, 'God is with us' (Matthew 1:23) – was only disclosed at Calvary, as God suffered with us and for us. God is with us in our pain and suffering.

The cross speaks to us of a 'God who is hidden in suffering' (Luther). It does not speak to us about – indeed, it forbids us to speak about – the elimination of suffering and pain through obedience to the will of God. At Calvary, God entered into the darkness of human pain and suffering. God faced the threat of extinction – and having met it, having recognised, exposed and named it as it really is, he conquered it. What was once meaningless and pointless, an inevitable and ineliminable aspect of human existence, becomes charged with meaning – it is made glorious and redemptive, it is lent dignity, because it was this pain and suffering that God turned into an instrument of deliverance and transformation. So dark was our situation that God himself had to enter and occupy it in order to make it light. In the very experience which man has come to regard as meaningless, threatening and inevitable, God chose to identify with him. God knows and experiences human suffering and pain at first hand. Just as we are made in God's image and likeness (Genesis 1:26–27), so we share in his sufferings and passion. Being made in the image of God carries with it the invitation to share in the divine suffering. The words of Luther bear reflection:

> A theologian of the cross (that is, someone who speaks of the crucified and hidden God) teaches that suffering, the cross and death are the most precious treasure of all, and the most sacred relics which the Lord of this theology has himself consecrated and blessed, not just by the touch of his most holy flesh, but also by the embrace of his most holy and divine will. And he has left these relics here to be kissed, sought after, and embraced. How fortunate and blessed is anyone who is considered by God to be so worthy that these treasures of Christ should be given to him!

The theology of the cross invites us to consider evil and suffering as they really are, at last unmasked, and in that experience to recognise the redeeming love of God towards us. We experience forgiveness by being shown our sin as we have never seen it before, just as it is impossible for us to experience the love of God without deepening our awareness of the suffering and pain which attend it.

It is at this point that a further point should be made. Against what God is 'protest atheism' directed? What 'God' are we actually talking about? Earlier we noted the classic understanding of God as an omnipotent, eternal, change-less being remote from the world. This understanding of God is often referred to as 'classical theism'. The signifi-cance of 'protest atheism' is that it appears to be directed against *this* understanding of God – in other words, *atheism* is basically *anti-theism*. According to the classical theist tradition, God cannot suffer. According to the Christian tradition Jesus Christ, as God and man, suffered and died upon the cross. The cross, by its very existence, forces us to look hard at the concept of God with which we are working – for we cannot simultaneously and uncritically amalga-mate these two concepts of God. We must either abandon the classical theist conception of God or else abandon the thesis that the cross is the central and decisive locus for our knowledge of God. To do the latter involves violating the integrity of the Christian tradition, forcing us to adopt the former course of action – and by doing so, to eliminate an unhelpful and positively misleading influence upon our thinking about God.

The inadequacies of the 'classical theist' position have long been known. For the French philosopher and math-ematician Pascal, it was necessary to encounter the 'God of Abraham, Isaac and Jacob, not the God of the philos-ophers'. Because God never changes, he never does any-thing – he shows no signs of life and is to all intents and purposes dead. The Christian tradition unhesitatingly speaks of a God who *loves* sinners, and it is not prepared to surrender this hard-won insight because the God of classi-cal theism cannot be said to 'love' in any meaningful sense of the term. The Christian tradition is saturated with the idea of a God who *acts*, who *loves*, who *gives* – and who *suffers*. This idea is far removed from Aristotle's Unmoved Mover (unmoved emotionally as well as physically!) who is wholly unconscious of the world, serene and unmoved by its pain and suffering.

There has been a growing suspicion in the past decades that it is the God of classical theism which has led to the cul-de-sac of modern atheism, and which has exerted a stranglehold upon authentically *Christian* reflection upon God for far too long. These insights are not new: Luther stood at the end of a series of medieval writers highly critical of the distortion of the concept of God due to Aristotelian influence. In the 'crucified and hidden God' – the God of the theology of the cross, the God of Calvary – we are provided with a weapon by which we may liberate ourselves from the oppression of both classical theism and the forms of atheism which have arisen in response to it.

An example of this oppression may be helpful. Consider the age-old question: If God is totally good and omnipotent, why does he permit suffering? Time and time again, this question is discussed in the philosophy journals in the terms laid down by classical theism, with results which can only greatly assist the advance of atheism. But what is meant by the terms of the question – for example, what is meant by 'good'? what is meant by 'omnipotent'? Are there not certain specifically *Christian* insights into these terms, which differ radically from those of classical theism? Let us develop this point with reference to the idea of *omnipotence*. What does it mean to say that God is 'omnipotent'? For the classical theist, it means that God is free to do anything, provided logical contradiction doesn't result. Thus the fact that God can't make a three-sided square is not seen as a threat to his omnipotence. But otherwise, he can do anything. To give an example: God is free to create the universe – and he is equally free not to create the universe. He has the ability to do either – but not both, obviously.

But the God of the Christian tradition is a God who *acts*, rather than a God who surveys possibilities open to him. Once God has decided to create, the option of *not* creating is no longer open to him. And once God has committed himself to a given course of action, he excludes actualisation of something which nevertheless may be logically possible. For example, consider these two possibilities:

1 To become man
2 Not to become man.

The actualisation of possibility 1 excludes possibility 2 – but this does not arise from any lack of omnipotence on God's part! In fact it arises through the exercise of precisely that omnipotence! More importantly, if God *is* omnipotent, he must be at liberty to set that omnipotence aside, and voluntarily to impose certain restrictions upon his course of action – to put it dramatically, but effectively, he must be free to have his hands tied behind his back. The *Christian* understanding of the omnipotence of God is that of a God *who voluntarily places limitations upon his course of action*. The God of classical theism contemplates possibilities which always remain open precisely because he never does anything: the 'crucified and hidden God' *acts* – and by acting eliminates possibilities which would otherwise be open.

For the Christian, God voluntarily submitted himself to the humiliation and shame of the cross. Although he was under no external obligation to do so, he freely set aside his omnipotence. He whom we could never capture gave himself up to the nails of the cross. And so it was that the glory of the omnipotent Lord of all creation gave himself up to the shame and powerlessness of the cross. The hands that flung the stars into the heavens were surrendered to the nails of the cross. In the wreckage of the classical theist concept of 'divine omnipotence' we are given an insight into the way in which God has chosen to operate. And we must learn to come to terms with this concept of 'omnipotence', because it is revealed to us in the cross as the model by which we must both understand God and exercise authority within his church. The 'omnipotence' in question is not that defined by the logic of the situation, but as disclosed in the cross. We are not given a model of God as the omnipotent Lord, but as the servant king. It is this God whom the church proclaims to the world in the 'preaching of the cross' – to which we now turn.

6 THE PREACHING OF THE CROSS

At the centre of the Christian proclamation of Christ – the
'word of the cross' (1 Corinthians 1:18) – lies an *existential
challenge*: a direct and immediate challenge to those who
hear to reorientate their hearts and minds towards the
person of Jesus Christ. It is a challenge which has been
passed down through the ages by the Christian tradition,
until it confronts us today. The Christian preaching of the
cross consists of an irreversible intermingling of historical
and theological truth-affirmations – the assertion that God
encounters us in the cross of Jesus Christ, with the capacity
to transform our existence.

In the preaching of the cross the church's memory of the
event of the cross is brought into the present in order that
this event may be re-presented to those who hear the word
of the cross and that its existential challenge be reaffirmed.
The continued existence of the Christian church depends
upon its ability to call a generation which is yet unborn to
faith in an unseen God through its preaching of the crucified Christ. In the present chapter we are concerned with
identifying the relevance of the cross to this Christian
preaching and establishing a theological basis to the act of
preaching itself.

For Paul, the basis of Christian preaching and mission
was the 'word of the cross', the proclamation to those
outside the community of faith of the possibility of a
redemptive and transforming encounter with the living
God here and now. Underlying the 'word of the cross' is the
fundamental assumption that human language, despite all
its weaknesses and shortcomings, may not merely point
beyond itself to the greater reality of the living God, but

may become a means by which God encounters and confronts humanity.

Faith comes from hearing, and the associated process of understanding (Romans 10:14–17). Although human words are incapable in themselves of encapsulating God, of reducing God to manageable proportions, they establish a framework within which the living God may himself be encountered. The 'word of the cross' is not to be identified with God – it points beyond itself to the greater personal reality underlying it. It identifies a pattern of divine presence and activity, supremely disclosed by the cross and resurrection, which both illuminates and transforms human existence. It invites its hearers to read this pattern of divine presence and activity into their own existence, to make the connection between the death and resurrection of Jesus Christ and their own situation. It is an invitation to read the story of our own lives in the light of the cross and resurrection, in order that we may realise that the 'word of the cross' addresses *us*. Through the proclamation of the 'word of the cross', each generation is brought back to the foot of that same cross, to be confronted afresh with its challenge and demand.

'Faith comes from what is heard, and what is heard comes by the preaching of Christ' (Romans 10:17 RSV). How does the 'theology of the cross' illuminate preaching? The importance of the point will be obvious. Christianity is not propagated biologically, nor is everyone a Christian. The suggestion that everyone is actually an 'anonymous Christian' is perhaps one of the most undignifying suggestions made in recent theological debate. To suggest that even those who have consciously decided to reject Christianity, in addition to those who are indifferent to its claims, are actually Christians, whether they know it or like it, is nothing less than an insult to their integrity and a perversion of the Christian proclamation. Faith is born through the hearing of the word, involving a response on our part. The expansion of the church – a necessary precondition for ensuring that Christian social and political insights are taken seriously by those who exercise power in society –

depends upon a revival of the sense of the mission of the church. Proclamation is the precondition for the fulfilment of the Christian social vision in western society, and any attempt on the part of the church to evade this point renders the vision of social transformation on the basis of such Christian insights potentially utopian. The 'preaching of Christ' holds the key to the expansion and consolidation of the church in the years which lie ahead, which in turn establishes its position to intervene for good in the western democratic tradition.

The vocabulary of preaching

We are told that it is impossible to make sense of the Christian proclamation in the modern period. There is undoubtedly some truth in this confident overstatement. But there is little truth in the conclusion which some have drawn from this observation – that the Christian proclamation is outdated and ought to be abandoned altogether or restated in purely secular terms which everyone can understand. Unfortunately, the secular meaning of the gospel is considerably less easy to discern than might be expected, and even the very modest results which this way of approaching the gospel yields are open to question. But perhaps most serious of all is the rather naive approach to language which this approach presupposes.

The meaning of a word is not totally given by the word itself, but is determined by its setting or context. The meaning of a word depends upon its setting. Some simple examples will bring this point out. I might ask a friend the following question: 'Did you win the set?' His answer to this question will depend upon what he thinks I mean by the word 'set'. For example, if I had been watching him play tennis, he would assume that this was the setting or context which gave the word 'set' its meaning – in which case he would tell me how his game of tennis was going. On the other hand he might have been taking part in a competition with two possible prizes – a silver tray or a set of china. In that case he would assume that I was asking him which of the two prizes he won. The principle involved is known as 'polysemy', which just means that a given word can bear a number of meanings – and, as we have seen, the meaning intended is usually given by the setting.

The same sort of thing is going on in many other situations. For example, you might be asked: 'Where are the points?' The meaning of this question is given by its context. You may be a railway signalman new to your job and anxious to make sure that you know where all your equipment is situated; you may be moving into a new house and anxious to find the electric power point to boil your electric kettle; you may be an irate teacher of classical Hebrew, irritated with a pupil for leaving out the vowel signs. This principle is familiar from everyday life: words bear different meanings in different situations, and we need to be clear about which context applies before attempting to use them.

This point has been emphasised by Ludwig Wittgenstein, who noted that 'to imagine a language means to imagine a form of life . . . The speaking of language is part of an activity, or of a form of life.' In other words, language is used to refer to things which are set within the context of the way of life of those who use that language. Two people who do not share the same way of life will inevitably find difficulty in understanding each other at points, simply because one may occasionally use words in a way which has no parallel within the other's experience.

To return to our example, noted above, concerning the word 'set' as used to refer to a game of tennis. Suppose a third person were listening to our conversation, who knew nothing of the rules of tennis, and wished to understand what a 'set' was. This individual might, for example, come from a culture in which tennis was totally unknown. In this case the use of the word 'set' in this context would remain completely meaningless to him unless the game of tennis were explained. And by explaining the game of tennis, the framework which gives the word 'set' its special 'tennis-meaning' is established. This individual could be taken to watch a game of tennis and hear the word 'set' used naturally in this context. In short, to understand the use of certain words (whether they are new words or familiar words used in a strange way) it is necessary to understand the framework which gives them their meaning. As Wittgenstein so correctly observes, the use of language is set within the framework of a way of life, and to understand that language it is necessary to understand that way of life.

With this in mind, consider the statement: 'Jesus saves.' The word 'saves' is already familiar from a number of contexts – for example, rescuing someone from drowning, or a goalkeeper preventing a ball from entering the goal. But this does not mean that 'Jesus rescues someone from drowning' or 'Jesus prevented the ball from entering the net.' It simply means that a word is being used in a specific setting or context, and is associated with a whole way of life, of understanding reality, which gives it that meaning. It may be that the way in which the same word is used in other contexts helps us understand its meaning in relation to Jesus – but the full meaning of the word is disclosed by the way of conceiving reality associated with the Christian tradition. In order to *explain* what the word 'saves' means, it is necessary to 'explain' the Christian world-view, and the specific function of the word 'saves' within this context. The problem is not solved by replacing the word 'saves' with some different word allegedly more intelligible to 'secular humanity' – because its meaning is not given by the word itself, but by the way in which it is used by Christians. As Wittgenstein pointed out, 'you learn the game by watching how others play' – and the way in which Christian words are used is to be learnt by understanding the meanings given to them by the Christian tradition.

That Christian tradition, from the New Testament onwards, is unequivocal on the central point that God intends the restoration of a lost world to himself, and that in Jesus Christ this intention is both expressed and made a genuine possibility. This central affirmation of God's redemptive activity in the cross and resurrection of Jesus Christ is, however, *addressed to the specific form which the human predicament takes*. If the form of 'lostness' experienced is that of captivity and slavery in an alien land, salvation is understood to involve liberation, an exodus to the homeland. If 'lostness' is experienced as material prosperity, perhaps coupled with social injustice, salvation is understood in terms of judgment and a call to repentance and social action. The universality of the gospel proclamation of salvation in Christ must be directed to the *specific situation* of its hearers – it must be made context-specific. The gospel proclamation is not addressed 'to whom it may concern', but to the specific forms taken by the human predicament. The preacher must know the situation of his audience and the relevance of his gospel to that situation if he is to bring out the full richness and relevance of the Christian proclamation for them. The complexity and diversity of the human situation is matched by a corresponding complexity in the understanding of salvation – with the fundamental insight being retained, that salvation is primarily about being restored to fellowship with God through the death and resurrection of Jesus Christ.

The meanings associated with words are usually brought out through what have come to be known as 'paradigm cases' or 'model cases'. In other words, you illustrate the way in which a word is used, and hence the meaning it bears, by giving examples of situations in which it is used. For example, a child may learn the meaning of the word 'save' by watching a television programme in which a drowning man is dragged from the sea by a lifeboat, or another in which a cat is rescued from a rocky ledge halfway down a cliff by a passing motorist. He learns that the word 'save' is appropriate to both situations, and begins to associate the word with situations in which individual humans or animals are extricated from dangerous situations. These are 'paradigm cases' which illustrate the meaning of the word.

Similarly, Christian vocabulary is learnt through paradigm cases. In scripture, the word 'save' is appropriate in two cases: the deliverance of the children of Israel from bondage in Egypt, and our deliverance from the fear of death and bondage to sin through the resurrection of Jesus

Christ from the dead. Both cases are stated in narrative form: in other words, they are stories – memorable stories, as it happens – through the 'telling' of which the Christian meaning of the word 'save' becomes apparent. It refers to an action of God in which some are delivered from a hostile or dangerous situation – and the assertion 'Jesus saves' may be understood without undue difficulty with reference to the 'paradigm case' of the crucifixion and resurrection of Jesus. Linguistically speaking, the significance of the crucifixion and resurrection of Jesus Christ is that it is the ultimate and normative 'paradigm case' for the vocabulary of Christianity – as we argued in an earlier chapter, even the word 'God' may be said to gain its full meaning from this paradigm case.

The suggestion that, because traditional Christian vocabulary has lost its meaning for those outside the church, it must be replaced with secular alternatives, may thus be seen to be quite unconvincing. The human race has always had a remarkable ability to adapt its language to deal with new situations, as the rapid rise of technology and its associated vocabulary has demonstrated. In the case of the Christian vocabulary, the words used gain their characteristic meaning from the paradigm case of the crucifixion and resurrection of Jesus Christ – a historical event, already stated in narrative form. The rehearsing of the resurrection of the crucified Jesus provides in itself the basis of the crucial transition between the *event* of the cross and the *word* of the cross, by establishing the framework within which words such as 'save' may be used.

To become a Christian is to learn a new language, or at least to give a new meaning to an old one. The church and her preachers must recognise this difficulty, but they need hardly feel overwhelmed by it. The history of the proclamation of Christianity in the Hellenist environment of the first century indicates that, despite all the conceptual and semantic difficulties encountered, the 'word of the cross' was charged with a significance and power which was able to overcome even these barriers. A more recent example may help illustrate this point.

The eighteenth- and nineteenth-century European missionaries to India found their evangelistic ministries seriously hindered by a number of factors. First, many inadvertently confused western European morals with Christianity, and accidentally placed an unnecessary – and virtually insuperable! – obstacle in the path of their hearers. Second, many of them found difficulty in expressing some New Testament terms in the vernacular Indian languages, and were thus unable to explain Christianity at a conceptual level. The experience of the Serampore mission in early nineteenth-century Bengal was, however, highly instructive. The simple narration of the passion, death and resurrection of Jesus Christ was found to possess a remarkable power. Even though it was difficult to draw out the full significance of this narrative, due to linguistic problems, the story itself proved adequate as a basis of the Christian proclamation. The narrative of the crucifixion and resurrection established the framework which gave meaning to the terms these missionaries subsequently used to tease out its meaning. Then as now, the preacher must learn to gain confidence not in his own ability to preach but in the power of the gospel and in the God who raised Jesus Christ from the dead. For in the end, it is God's gospel, and we must assume that if God can raise Christ from the dead, he can deal equally decisively with the relatively minor problems associated with communicating this fact and its significance – which is not to underestimate the size of the problem, only to put it in perspective.

The content of the Christian proclamation takes the form of words, but its subject is not to be identified with them – underlying the words, ideas and concepts is the greater reality of the living God himself, to whom the proclamation points. Like John the Baptist, it points to something greater than itself, to something *different*, to a *person* whom we are given to understand we are about to encounter. To develop this point, we need to consider the implications of speaking of God as a person.

The proclamation of the crucified Christ

Ideas may be defined in words, where persons may merely be described. The Christian tradition has always insisted that it is possible to encounter the living God in a real and recognisable manner, here and now, while maintaining a certain eschatological reserve – in other words, acknowledging that we only meet God face to face in heaven. 'For now we see in a mirror dimly, but then face to face. Now I know in part; then I shall understand fully' (1 Corinthians 13:12 RSV). The Christian experience down the centuries is that God is to be thought of in personal terms – an idea expressed with some force in parables such as that of the prodigal son.

When dealing with persons, we are dealing with a category which cannot be reduced to propositional statements. To put this more briefly: persons are irreducible. Let us illustrate this point before exploring its relevance to the proclamation of the word of the cross. Let us consider how we come to know another person – let us say, a person called 'Peter Smith'. We can make the following statements about him:

1 He is male
2 He was aged forty-five last birthday
3 He likes listening to baroque music.

And so we could go on – we could list his height, his weight, his social security number, and so on. And all of these would be true statements – but none of them are good enough to tell us *what he is like as a person*. All of us know only too well how very different a person turns out to be when we meet them, even when we think we know a lot about them beforehand! So the first point to be made is that it is very difficult, and probably impossible, to build up a picture of a person from statements about him – what you need to do is *encounter* the person and form your own impressions. So it is with God: we can make all sorts of statements about him – but, in the end, these don't help us visualise God as a person. We need to encounter him, meet him, experience him – and in this way, we come to know God.

This point can be brought out quite easily in the English language, which recognises a distinction between 'knowing' and 'knowing about' someone. You can know *about* someone without ever *knowing* them – just as most people know something about the President of the United States or the British Royal Family, without knowing them personally. Christianity asserts that we can *know*, and not just know *about*, God (see John 17:3). Statements about God are helpful, but are quite inadequate to express the personal reality who lies behind them – just as our statements about Peter Smith may help us prepare to meet him, but are no substitute for a personal encounter with him.

Let us now take this point further. Personal relationships are not static, they are dynamic – they develop. When we meet Peter Smith, we may find that we strike up a good relationship which develops into a close friendship – and that means that we are changed by Peter Smith, and he is changed by us. All of us know this from experience – how personal relationships change the people involved. Furthermore, it will be evident that different individuals will relate to Peter Smith in different ways – one of the great difficulties faced by biographers is the remarkably different impressions of their subject they gain from those who knew him, each reflecting a different aspect of that person.

The relevance of these observations to the preaching of the cross will be obvious. Merely to present the world with statements about God or interpretations of the meaning of the death and resurrection of Jesus Christ, is to preach *about* God – it is to *inform* our hearers. While education is an important part of preaching, it is not its chief part. The chief function of preaching is to re-present the cross, to establish a framework within which our hearers may realise the possibility of encountering the living God here and now – and thus to prepare the way for that encounter. And that encounter will transform our hearers' understanding of God, just as our understanding of Peter Smith is transformed through meeting him. The preacher's task is to prepare the way for the personal encounter of the individual with the living God, by proclaiming the necessity, the possibility and the actuality of that encounter. Like John the Baptist, he points to something greater than himself – the crucified Christ. In effect the preacher proclaims the nearness of God to his hearers and then directs them to where he may be found – in the crucified and risen Christ. Precisely because the personal reality of God lies behind the gospel, the preacher may avoid the mistake of thinking that he has to *argue* people into the kingdom of God, that he has to *persuade* them of the richness of God – his task is to point them to the place at which God makes himself available for us to encounter him, in the cross of Christ.

Merely to preach theories about the meaning of Christ is to present a reduced Christ to the world. For Paul, the function of the preacher is to 'proclaim Christ' (Philippians 1:15–18), just as a herald might proclaim the coming of his king. The preacher points away from himself, to the living reality which underlies his faith and his words, knowing that an encounter with this reality will confirm his proclamation. Precisely because Christianity is not about ideas or concepts, but about an encounter with the living God, the preacher has the task of *facilitating* this encounter, rather than justifying its existence in the first place. It is significant in this respect that much of the gospel narratives are taken up with recounting the impression which Jesus made upon individuals as he encountered them rather than with theories about his identity.

An analogy may help bring this (admittedly difficult) point out. In John's gospel, we find Philip telling Nathanael of the remarkable person he has just encountered: 'We have found him of whom Moses in the law and also the prophets wrote, Jesus of Nazareth, the son of Joseph' (John 1:45 RSV). Nathanael indicates that he is not inclined to take this judgment with any great seriousness, to which Philip replies, 'Come and see' (John 1:46 RSV). Nathanael then encounters Jesus himself, and through that encounter is himself moved to declare, 'Rabbi, you are the Son of God! You are the King of Israel!' (John 1:47–49 RSV). Philip here illustrates the true function of the preacher, of the one who proclaims Jesus Christ: he describes the perceived significance of Jesus, and then directs his hearers *to find out for themselves by a personal encounter with the one to whom he bears witness.*

As we saw earlier, it is impossible to describe or define a person in propositional terms – that definition is only arrived at through an encounter. The preacher must point to Jesus Christ, and invite his hearers to encounter this living reality for themselves by taking the leap of faith. The preacher draws upon his own experience and that of the Christian community down the ages in declaring that this leap of faith, this creative and transforming risk, leads to a redemptive encounter with the risen Christ. It is this encounter with the risen Christ, not the preacher's words themselves, which underlies and undergirds his proclamation. Those words testify to and attempt to describe a present encounter, and declare that this encounter is a present possibility for those who have yet to experience it. At this point the preacher's words point away from him to the source of that encounter, in an invitation to tap this spiritual source, to 'taste and see that the Lord is good' (Psalm 34:8 rsv), to encounter the living God where he makes himself available for us, in the cross of Jesus Christ.

This is not, of course, to say that interpretations of the identity and significance of the death and resurrection of Jesus Christ are unimportant: as we have argued consistently throughout this work, they are of central importance in that they are the essential foundation of the identity and relevance of the church. We are simply making the point, a point which is so easily overlooked – that Christians proclaim a *person*, not an *idea*. Ideas need to be defended, and tend to go out of fashion rather quickly – a person needs to be encountered, and the result of that encounter may be a lasting relationship. And the central question to be asked of the preacher is not, 'Why should I believe this idea?', but 'Where and how may I encounter this person?' And it is the task of the preacher to tell him where and how – by directing him to the cross and resurrection of Jesus Christ.

'When I came to you, brethren, I did not come proclaiming to you the testimony of God in lofty words or wisdom. For I decided to know nothing among you except Jesus Christ and him crucified' (1 Corinthians 2:1–2 rsv). It is here that God stoops to meet us, and we respond in faith.

Our understanding of the personal nature of our experience of God has been clarified in the present century through the works of Ferdinand Ebner, Martin Buber, and others influenced by their 'personalism' (as this philosophy has come to be known). Buber points out that we experience two very different relations in life: an *I-It* relation, or *experience*, in which we relate to something passive (such as a table), and an *I-You* relation, or *encounter*, in which we relate to something active (such as another person). In an *I-It* relation, we are always active, taking the initiative in establishing the relation, so that we may know more about the object in question. We always have the upper hand. But in an *I-You* relation, the situation is very different – because the other party to the relation is as active as we are, and may take the initiative away from us. While we are trying to find out about them, they may be trying to find out about us. But, most important of all, they may disclose themselves to us – we don't necessarily need to find out about them, because they may take that initiative away from us by disclosing themselves first. Although these insights are open to criticism at points, they have been appropriated by Christian theologians who have emphasised that God *encounters* us – he's not something passive which we experience, like an object. God takes the initiative away from us, by determining where and in what manner he will disclose himself to us – it is not something over which we have control.

The pivotal feature of the Christian faith – the encounter of the individual *here and now* with the living God through the crucified and risen Christ – can be expressed in, but not reduced to, human words. The word of proclamation is a catalyst, by which the possibility of an encounter with the 'God and Father of our Lord Jesus Christ' may be transformed into a present actuality. Human words are the earthen vessel conveying the treasure of the risen Christ. They are the carrier, the medium, for something much greater. In many respects the preacher is like John the Baptist, pointing away from himself to someone greater, to whom he bears witness. The power and vitality of the Christian proclamation derives not from the words used, but from the one who stands behind it – the risen Christ.

The wisdom of the cross

One of the many threads woven together by Paul in his celebrated exposition of the 'theology of the cross' is the personal inadequacy of himself as a preacher (1 Corinthians 1:17–2:5, especially 2:1–5). For Paul, the power and the appeal of his message lay neither in the person of the preacher, nor the eloquence of his speech, nor the wisdom of his words – but in the crucified and risen Christ. Luther described the crucified Christ as 'the wisdom which is folly to the world', in that the world sees only the external dimension or aspect of the event – a man dying helplessly, pointlessly, mocked by his enemies and abandoned by his friends, even God himself. Faith possesses the insight, denied to the world, which allows this event to be seen in a different light, from the standpoint of the resurrection. What the world regards as folly and weakness is demonstrated to be nothing other than the wisdom and strength of God. In the resurrection of the crucified Christ, God overturns the judgment of the world, and establishes the crucial insight that experience and faith tend to contradict one another.

The theme of the divine contradiction of the judgment of the world is essential to the theology of the cross. God does not endorse the judgment of the world, but contradicts it in order to force the world to reconsider the basis of its judgments. The supreme instance of this contradiction is the cross. The world looks at the cross from the standpoint of Good Friday; the believer looks upon it from the standpoint of Easter Day. The same event is seen in two very different perspectives. For the world, the cross spells death; for the believer, it spells life: for the world, the cross spells condemnation; for the believer, it spells vindication. The judgment of the world upon the dying Christ is overturned and inverted by God. And so the preacher, in confronting the world with the crucified Christ, must learn to expect that the world will regard this as scandalous or stupid (1 Corinthians 1:23). He will be tempted to embellish his proclamation of the word of the cross with what the world regards as wisdom. Yet it is the event of the cross itself which is the foundation of faith.

Humility is a virtue the academic theologian finds hard to learn, often identifying it with an uncritical submission to an external authority inconsistent with academic integrity. He would much rather be able to lay down the conditions upon which God might reveal himself or deduce the most appropriate form which this revelation might take or speculate on the nature of the God thus revealed. These possibilities have been excluded by the cross, and our answers to these questions are given to us, rather than deduced by us, in that same event. Human preconceptions of what God must be like are exposed by the cross as mere fictions of the human imagination – and the theological autonomy of the human intellect which engendered these preconceptions is thus challenged. God has revealed himself as he wishes to be known – and we must respond to this, rather than attempt to lay down the conditions under which God may reveal himself. The cross passes judgment upon the theological competence of human reason by demonstrating that what reason regards as folly hides the wisdom of God. The cross destroys the illusion that we know God adequately through our reason, and thus opens the way to 'true theology and the knowledge of God'. The recognition of the paradoxical and contradictory relation between human and divine wisdom opens the way to our turning away from our confidence in our reason to understand God and our strength to turn to him – and by doing so, we eliminate the obstacles in the path of God. God destroys before he may build – destroying our preconceptions of what he is like, and what we ourselves are capable of, in order to bring us back to him. The English poet John Donne expressed a similar sentiment thus:

> Batter my heart, three-personed God; for you
> As yet but knock, breathe, shine and seek to mend;
> That I may rise, and stand, o'erthrow me, and bend
> Your force, to break, blow, burn and make me new.
> I, like a usurped town, to another due,
> Labour to admit you, but oh, to no end,
> Reason your viceroy in me, me should defend,
> But is captived, and proves weak or untrue,
> Yet dearly I love you, and would be loved fain,
> But am betrothed unto your enemy,
> Divorce me, untie, or break that knot again,
> Take me to you, imprison me, for I
> Except you enthrall me, never shall be free,
> Nor ever chaste, except you ravish me.

The history of Christian thought demonstrates how secular philosophies have consistently been used as a vehicle for the Christian proclamation. Platonism, Aristotelian, Hegelianism, existentialism – all have, in their day and age, been adapted and exploited to further the end of the proclamation of the gospel. As Alfred North Whitehead so wisely remarked, 'Christianity is a religion seeking a metaphysic.' This clearly has enormous apologetic value, in that the preacher may exploit similarities between Christianity and the world-view of his hearers in order to proclaim the gospel more effectively, using such similarities as 'points of contact' for his proclamation. The theology of the cross forces us not to reject the use of such philosophies but to be critical in doing so. The gospel is not to be *identified with* any of these systems. In particular, two points must be made.

First, the fall of these systems does not entail the fall of Christianity. It has often been observed that philosophies are abandoned, rather than disproved, as intellectual fashions change. Christianity may, for apologetic reasons, exploit points of these systems as 'vehicles' for conveying distinctively *Christian* truth – but that does not mean that the truth of Christianity is dependent upon the truth of these systems. The kernel of the gospel may clothe itself with various husks – Platonic, Aristotelian and Hegelian, for instance – in the course of history: the essential point is to avoid confusing kernel and husk. Furthermore, the fact that Christianity is inconsistent with these systems at points cannot be interpreted as implying that in these matters Christianity is *wrong* – merely that Christianity and that 'philosophy' do not agree over those precise issues. Every day and age has its favourite philosophies, on the basis of which some judge Christianity and find it wanting by their standards – but a survey of the history of thought demonstrates just how rapidly many of these systems rise and fall, and raises the question of why theologians should feel obliged to try and defend the Christian faith in the face of such an ephemeral challenge. Tactically, it is clearly of importance to mount such a defence – but strategically, it would seem to serve little purpose. In the short term it is helpful to demonstrate that Christianity can hold its own in the face of idealism or logical positivism – but in the long term the threat posed by such systems is eliminated by the passage of time itself.

Second, the fact that Christianity may exploit certain aspects of, for example, Platonism, does not mean that Christianity is obliged to accept as axiomatic every Platonic insight, and alter its self-understanding accordingly. Christianity must maintain its essential distinctiveness, grounded and rooted in the cross and resurrection, unless its exploitation of secular wisdom is to become its reduction to a religious version of a secular philosophy. By insisting that the cross is the internal criterion of the Christian faith, this danger may be minimised – but the history of Christian thought provides all too many instances for comfort of the reduction of Christianity to the secular intellectual system then in fashion.

Christ's pulpit is his cross: it is from the cross that he addresses the world. The same cross that made disciples into apostles is re-presented and re-enacted through the proclamation of the word of the cross to a disbelieving world. Charged with a wisdom and power of its own, the logic of the cross addresses us amidst the contradictions and confusion of human experience, casting light upon it and offering to transform it. Directing our attention away from what the world regards as wise, we learn a new wisdom, a new logic, of death transformed into life, despair into hope, and darkness into light. This is no demand to commit intellectual suicide, but is a plea to encounter God as he has made himself known to us.

The word of the cross and culture

The proclamation of the word of the cross does not take place in a vacuum, but in a specific historical context. If that proclamation is to transcend this specific situation, it must be capable of freeing itself from the cultural constraints which that situation places upon it. In other words the proclamation of the word of the cross is addressed to a cultural situation, and may be accommodated to it – but it is neither restricted to, nor to be identified with, that situation. There is, as there always has been, a danger that the Christian proclamation will be overwhelmed by the prevailing culture, and eventually be submerged within it, unable to recover its sense of identity and relevance. To many historians of Christian thought, Liberal Protestantism appears to represent an example of precisely this situation: Christianity was identified with a culture to such a point that it appeared incapable of distinguishing itself from it. With the collapse of that optimistic culture through the impact of the First World War came the simultaneous collapse of that theology. In this case the Christian proclamation was trapped within a cultural situation and appeared to many to be incapable of extricating itself from it.

The difficulty facing the preacher is that he wishes to address himself to a specific situation without so linking his proclamation to that situation that it loses its points of contact with and relevance for other cultural situations. In particular, three situations of potential difficulty may be noted.

First, *cultural changes arising through the worldwide propagation of Christianity*. As is well known, the early British missionaries to both India and China tended to confuse Christianity and contemporary British bourgeois culture, with the result that the indigenisation of Christianity was seriously impaired. Through an uncritical, if well-meaning, absorption of cultural parameters into the gospel proclamation, the missionaries succeeded in emphasising the foreign character of the gospel to their hearers. Numerous difficulties arose through the imposition of British cultural norms upon Indian society, under the mistaken apprehension that these were *Christian* values. This difficulty has, of course, long since been recognised, and there is every indication that the need to disinvest the gospel proclamation of hidden cultural values has been well taken.

The theology of the cross forces us to investigate the hidden extent of the accommodation of the Christian proclamation to the cultural norms and values of the community from which that proclamation originates. Presuppositions, particularly ethical and social axioms, which we accept without question in the western liberal democracies and incorporate (perhaps unconsciously) into our proclamation of the gospel, may render that proclamation sterile to its hearers – not through any deficiency in the 'word of the cross', but through the naivete of the proclaimer. The cross forces us to be critical – not to *reject* the incorporation of cultural elements into our proclamation, but to be *aware* that this is what we are doing. Peripheral cultural elements must be identified in order that they may not be allowed to assume the status of essential elements of the proclamation and so they may be eliminated and replaced with elements deriving from a different cultural situation where this is appropriate.

The second difficulty relates to *different subcultures within a single society*. Most western societies are highly stratified, with the different strata tending to adopt different cultural norms and values. Thus in England, there are obvious differences between middle class and working class, between northern and southern culture and values, even though some suggest that these differences are gradually being eliminated through the homogenisation of society. Similar or comparable differences are evident in most societies. It will be obvious that the preacher accustomed to working within, shall we say, a northern English working-class urban community will absorb, probably unconsciously, the values and aspirations of that cultural situation – and should he subsequently be called upon to proclaim the gospel in a southern English middle-class commuter village, it is probable that his uncritical absorption of this ethos will seriously hinder, if not totally prejudice, that proclamation. It is quite common for the uncritical assumption of the superiority of one culture over another to result in the proclamation of cultural values, loosely integrated with a culturally-reduced version of the gospel. What the southern middle-class commuters *hear* their visiting preacher say (although he may not consciously have articulated such thoughts) is that he wished that they would all become northern, working class and urban.

The relative merits of cultures and subcultures are disputed, and some would suggest that an attempt to assess them is quite unacceptable, involving assumptions which approach those leading to cultural tyranny. There is an understandable tendency for the preacher to come – implicitly and even unconsciously – to regard his own cultural situation, whatever that may be, as normative. The preacher is simply not in a position to pass judgments upon a culture: his task is to ensure that the gospel becomes rooted within that culture, unimpeded by his own personal taste and predilections. Historically, Christianity has transformed culture from within – and where it has passed judgment upon a culture from outside, without being rooted in that culture, it has tended, if anything, to reinforce that culture in its previous views. One might reasonably ask whether converts on the traditional missionary fields of the last century were distinguished by their appropriation of the culture – whether American or western European – of those who proclaimed the gospel to them. The theology of the cross demands that an indigenous, a *local*, theology should be developed – not merely through the missionary dying to his own culture, but through his converts bringing *their* culture to the cross for it to be judged.

The third difficulty arises through *the inexorable passage of time, and the changes in cultural values within a society as a result*. The gospel must not be allowed, through its identification with the values of one particular moment in time, to be trapped in a time warp. The form which the gospel took in Victorian England cannot be held up as normative for all time, for example. There is every danger that a generation gap will arise in Christianity at least as serious as that observed in secular society, through the inability of those charged with the responsibility of proclaiming the gospel to break free from the cultural presuppositions of their youth. The church leaders of today tend to have become trapped in a theological time warp – they often seem unable to break free from the culturally-conditioned theology they absorbed as students, with the result that, though time passes, their theology remains rooted in a culture now dying or already dead. Times change, and we must change with them – not in the gospel we proclaim, but in the manner in which we accommodate it to each and every situation as it arises, and purge it of elements arising from previous attempts to accommodate it which are no longer regarded as helpful. We may learn from the past – but we may never return to it. Otherwise, Christianity will rapidly become an exhibit in the museum of the history of ideas.

We shall continue our discussion of the relation of the cross and culture in the remaining chapters. But its importance in relation to the subject of the proclamation of the cross will be evident. The very survival, let alone the expansion, of Christianity depends upon its capacity, mediated by people such as ourselves, to address the human situation directly, here and now. The central affirmation is that of an event – an event charged with meaning, power and vitality, which may be re-presented and re-enacted throughout human history. The Christian church must become a witness in the midst of contemporary secular society to the transforming action of the living God made known in the saving events which are narrated and interpreted in scripture and the Christian tradition, culminating in the cross and resurrection. The Christian church needs to recover its sense of mission along with its sense of identity in that cross, in the light of the illumination and transformation of the human situation which it brings.

In western society the Christian church has lost much of its secular power, and has yet to find a role – and yet that very role has been given to her, perhaps as her most precious heritage, by the risen Christ: 'Go . . . and make disciples of all nations' (Matthew 28:19 RSV). It is to her that the word of the cross has been entrusted, and it is time that confidence in that heritage was regained. At a time when the church seems to have nothing to offer society other than what society can do for itself, there is a pressing need for the church to grasp the opportunity of this moment by reappraising her role and reclaiming that which was originally given to her – the bearer of the word of the cross, the starting point for a new vision of humanity and society. To recall the words of Goethe:

> What you received as an inheritance,
> Make now your own, in order to use it!

In the following chapters, we shall consider the relevance of this Christian 'inheritance' of the theology of the cross for the life of the individual believer and of the Christian church.

7 LIFE UNDER THE CROSS: THE BELIEVER

For Paul, the scandalous enigma of the cross dominates the life of the individual believer. It is here that the paradoxes of Christian existence converge to form a pattern which, once recognised, enables the believer to relate the paradoxes of his own existence to the enigma of the cross. It is in the scandal of the cross that we learn that God's power comes to its full strength in and through weakness (2 Corinthians 12:9). It is through the pattern of divine presence in the suffering of Christ upon that cross that we realise that God's presence is to be seen in the believer's experience of suffering, which now assumes the character of a testimony to his sharing in Christ's riches (Romans 8:17; 2 Corinthians 1:5; 4:7–5:5). Suffering and death are recognised as the necessary complement to the new life of the believer, as he experiences the tension between the 'already' and the 'not yet' of the resurrection. It is through dying to himself and to the world that the believer rises to life with Jesus Christ (Romans 6:2–4; Galatians 2:19; Colossians 3:3). In this chapter we shall consider the bearing of the cross on the life of the believer. First, we must emphasise the scandal of the cross.

The scandal of the cross

From its birth until the present day, the Christian faith was and is distinguished from all other religions and ideologies by its worship of the crucified Christ. The taunt of the early opponents of Christianity was that believers worshipped 'an evil man and his cross' (*homo noxius et crux eius*). The very fact that Christians worshipped a man who had been crucified was sufficient to utterly discredit their beliefs in the eyes of Caecilius (a character in Minucius Felix' dialogue *Octavius*): 'The fact that their ceremonies centre on a man who was put to death for his crime on the deadly wood of the cross is to assign to these abandoned wretches sanctuaries which are appropriate to them, and the kind of worship which they deserve.' The same contempt is evident from a second-century Roman graffito, depicting a figure with the head of an ass being crucified, with a second figure standing alongside with an arm raised. The slogan accompanying this graffito is 'Alexamenos worships his god.'

The word of the cross was indeed folly to those who heard it proclaimed – a scandal which seemed to discredit the entire system of beliefs based upon it for that very reason. The passage of time has perhaps made it difficult for the modern reader to appreciate the sheer scandal and outrage caused to many by the first Christians' suggestion that God was revealed in the shame of the cross. Writing in the second century, Justin Martyr recorded the offence caused to the sophisticated citizens of Alexandria and elsewhere by the 'madness' of the Christian proclamation of the crucified Christ. The proclamation of the word of the cross was recognised as scandalous, offensive and deeply disturbing by those who heard it, for it represented a demand that they worship and adore a man executed in the most unseemly manner.

The reactions of the early opponents of Christianity bring home to us something which the passage of time has tended to dull and blunt – the sheer scandal of the cross. Perhaps it is those outside the church who realise how central and how apparently perverse the Christian claim actually is – for it is centred upon the crucified Christ. Those who regard religion as a matter of aesthetics, ethics or the science of the human spirit find themselves scandalised by the sheer perversity of this Christian symbol and attempt to eliminate it and substitute something more acceptable in its

place. But history will not permit the cross to be marginalised in this way. The first Christians saw in the scandal of
the cross the birth of new life, and based their interpretation
of God and the world upon it.

Faith was born as the night of the crucifixion gave way to
the dawn of the resurrection. Faith recognised in the crucifixion and resurrection a pattern of divine presence and
activity – and discerned this same pattern in the panorama
of human existence. In the defeat of Good Friday faith
acknowledged God's victory over death in the midst of
death and claimed this victory as its own. Faith recognised
in the cross the facing, naming, disarming and forgiveness
of human sin and claimed this forgiveness as its own. It
recognised in the dying Christ none other than the crucified
God making his appeal to us, demonstrating the full and
overwhelming extent of the love of God for sinful humans –
and responded to that love. In short, faith recognised in the
cross the key to life and salvation, and claimed that life and
salvation as its own.

In the course of its history the Christian tradition – like a
snowball rolling down a hill – accumulated material in
addition to that already present as its centre and nucleus.
The growing desire on the part of Christian apologists to
accommodate their faith to the aesthetic and moral presuppositions of their contemporaries inevitably meant that the
sheer scandal of the cross became diminished. To use
Goethe's famous illustration, the cross became 'wreathed
with roses' – cultural sensitivity, romanticism and sen-
timentality combined to change the harshness of the cross
into a symbol of gentleness. The scandal and folly of the
cross were set aside, as layers of accumulated tradition
surrounded that cross with interpretations which it had
never before possessed, allowing Christianity to clothe
itself in more splendid garments than the rags in which it
was born. Christianity began to gain a sense of dignity and
self-awareness as one of the most important phenomena of
world history – and overlooked the basis upon which that
phenomenon was born. Christianity began to view itself as
one of the most important social and ethical movements in

history – and ceased to ask itself the crucial questions concerning its identity and relevance.

And yet today, as those social and ethical insights are called into question by the secular world, and as the great theories of historical development begin to falter in the light of obvious degeneration, a new opportunity has arisen – the opportunity to purge the Christian quest for identity and relevance of this accumulated intellectual baggage, and return to the origin, the primal event, of faith. More and more, Christianity is being forced, through external and internal pressures, to abandon its intellectual, cultural and ethical pretensions, and to return to the cross – the cross of scandal and folly, disinvested of the tradition which allowed us to marginalise it. Today, perhaps more than ever, the cross is emerging from its shadowy existence as a symbol to assume its rightful place as the foundation and criterion of Christian faith. The inner dynamic of the Christian tradition is what it was given, and what it was shaped by, at its birth. Today we are confronted with a real and radical possibility – to rediscover and reforge the theology of the cross, to re-enter the despair of Good Friday in order to discover the joy of Easter Day and the hope of the Christian proclamation – to return to the apostolic faith, and the proclamation of the cross without the hindrance of the accumulated debris of inauthentic cultural tradition. Christianity and the faith of the individual believer alike may only be rejuvenated on the basis of its own origins. The renewal of both the corporate faith of the community and the personal spirituality of the individual depends upon a willingness to embrace and love the scandal of the cross.

Faith in the cross

To return to the cross is to return via the New Testament to the source of Christian faith. The New Testament is the title deed of the Christian faith, the classic expression of what Christians believe, and the witness to Christian faith and commitment from its very beginnings. It is there that we encounter the narrative of the event of the cross and its meaning – the assertion that God does not merely demonstrate his love through the cross, but gives effect to it in human history; the assertion that God enters the flux of human history, rides on its rage, rules its flood and changes its course from within. It also confronts us with a demand – the demand for faith.

The demand for faith is above all a demand that the hand of God be recognised in the resurrection of the one who was crucified. In this action, God overturned the judgment of the world, and with it exposed as idols its standards of righteousness, wisdom and power. The cross confronts us with the demand to turn away from the present age with its standards and values – which, when greatly magnified, lead to the 'God of this present age' – and instead bring our thinking about God, ourselves and his world into conformity with the cross. It was none other than God himself who raised Christ from the dead, thus vindicating and stamping with his seal of approval both Christ's person and his mission. The sense of wondering joy evoked by the resurrection is linked by the New Testament writers, particularly Paul, with the recognition that we, as individuals, are involved in Christ's death and resurrection. Through faith, the believer is placed in such a relation to Christ that all that happened in and through Christ's death and resurrection may be repeated in that individual, here and now.

Faith recognises the hand of God in the crucifixion and resurrection, and appropriates its power. Faith transfers the history of Jesus Christ from outside our personal existence to within it, making it an essential and integral part of our living and dying. The same enemies defeated upon the cross are those to be defeated in the believer's life: the power of death and sin, the apparent meaninglessness of human suffering, the oppression of the individual by the state and his fellow humans. In the great act of self-identification with us when he stepped on to the cross, Christ entered the sphere of sin's penalty and the horror of sin's curse, in order that he might engage with and disarm these age-old enemies.

But it is here that faith takes the step which experience forbids: it looks at the crucifixion from the standpoint of the resurrection. The resurrection is recognised as being the proclamation of a hidden victory, rather than the reversal of an open defeat. Like the Old Testament prophets, faith sees the outcome of the present situation, and interprets the situation in that light. It sees evil as defeated, whereas it remains a reality in experience. It sees human suffering as the point at which God draws closest to man, whereas we experience him as absent. It sees death swallowed up in victory, whereas death is experienced as victor. In all these things, faith views reality from the standpoint of the resurrection – and recognises the same pattern of divine activity and presence. Faith views the battleground of existence from a high peak, recognising in this battle precisely the same patterns as a battle once fought at Calvary, and interpreting it in that light.

For the thinkers of the Enlightenment, faith was a lower form of knowledge. You might believe that the world was flat, or that the earth revolved round the sun – but you weren't sure. And faith gives way to knowledge: science is able to demonstrate that the world isn't flat, and that the earth does indeed revolve around the sun. Faith now no longer remains: the belief that the earth is flat is demonstrated to be wrong, and the belief that the earth revolves around the sun is shown to be right – and neither are 'beliefs' any more. One is a falsehood, and the other a fact. Similarly, the Enlightenment tended to regard Christian faith as a lower form of knowledge, making statements about God and man which could not be verified, and which became redundant once philosophy had turned its omnicompetent attention to them. Thus Christian theologians tended to be regarded as intellectual flat-earthers.

With the recognition of the 'fiduciary rootedness of all reality' (Polanyi), this understanding of faith has given way to another – a pattern or way of looking at the world which allows us to make sense of it. As we have already discussed this point in an earlier chapter, we do not propose to repeat what has already been said – but we do wish to draw attention to the fact that the pattern disclosed by the crucifixion and resurrection of Jesus Christ lies at the heart of Christian faith. The 'fiduciary rootedness' of the Christian understanding of God's presence and activity within the world is grounded in the pattern disclosed by the resurrection of the one who was crucified. It is this pattern or framework which gives Christianity its distinctive approach to reality, in that this pattern is regarded as disclosing something much greater which is otherwise beyond our grasp – the manner in which God deals with his creation. The distinctive shape of reality, as conceived by the Christian, is given by the cross. It is increasingly being recognised that all of us create and live within mental pictures of reality – and the Christian's picture of reality is cruciform.

Understanding and obedience

For the Christian, 'truth' is not primarily about logical propositions or statements, but about an encounter with the living God himself, and the consequent struggle to try and put into words that greater reality. It is an unequal struggle. Commenting on Jacob's struggle with the angel at Peniel (Genesis 32:24–31), Thomas Aquinas drew attention to the difficulties facing the theologian as he wrestled with God:

> The whole night they wrestled, muscles straining, neither yielding; but at dawn the angel disappeared, apparently leaving the field clear to his opponent. But then Jacob felt a sharp pain in his thigh. He was left wounded and limping. And so it is with the theologian as he grapples with the mystery when God confronts him with it. He is taut, like a bent bow, grappling with human language; he struggles like a wrestler; he even seems to gain the upper hand. But then he feels a weakness, a weakness which is at once painful and delicious, for to be thus defeated is in fact the proof that his combat was divine.

All too often, theology becomes reduced to shadow-boxing, a wrestling with ideas and concepts, where in their place we should seek to wrestle with the living God. For God is not the object of theology, as we might scrutinise an amoeba at our leisure under our control in a laboratory, but is an untamed and untameable subject who stands over and against us, challenging our attempts to define and describe him. The Christian theologian is confronted with the mystery of the living God in the cross of Jesus Christ, and is obliged to recognise that this is a mystery which he can never master, but to which he must surrender. And as the story of Jacob indicates, wrestling with God is painful. Jacob was wounded by his struggle with God, just as we are wounded by our knowledge of God, which brings home to us our infidelity and sinfulness.

A further point must be made in relation to the term 'truth' itself. The Christian tradition has recognised that the 'truth' conveyed in the self-revelation of God is not simply objective, something which may be stated propositionally. This is not to say that such statements may not be made: it is simply to recognise that concepts such as 'faithfulness' – the enactment by word and deed of God's faithfulness to himself and to humanity – are elements which cannot be eliminated from our understanding of 'truth', as applied to God. Thus the Greek translation of the Old Testament – the Septuagint – renders the Hebrew word *emet* as *aletheia* (truth) on 119, and as *pistis* (faithfulness) on 26 occasions. Both ideas are contained within the same word. The 'truth which will set us free' (John 8:32) is not some abstract propositional or conceptual knowledge, but Jesus Christ himself (John 8:36), the concrete personal expression of God's faithfulness to himself and his redemptive promises towards us. The truth into which Jesus Christ leads us is the truth of God's faithfulness and reliability towards us, of steadfastness towards his own word, or the trustworthiness of his promises – and a corresponding demand for a concrete faithfulness, expressed in word and deed, on our part.

'Truth' is thus orientated towards living, towards a lifestyle, rather than towards intellectual assent to propositions. The antithesis of 'truth' is not so much 'error' as 'faithlessness', a failure to maintain faithfulness to the God who has demonstrated his faithfulness towards us in the crucifixion and resurrection of Jesus Christ. The theme of the 'truth of the cross' is thus not merely concerned with the theological analysis of the event of the cross and resurrection, but also with the recognition of the faithfulness of God towards sinful humanity, culminating in the events of the first Good Friday and Easter Day. It is concerned with action as much as with reflection; it is concerned with God's faithfulness towards us and his demand for faithfulness from us. It is a demand for action in our lives and lifestyles, embracing all of our existence, an ethical as much as a theological concept. The 'truth of the cross' is God's faithfulness to his promises of redemption for his people, expressed both in word and in deed, and places upon that people the obligation to respond in faithfulness to him.

The cross does not present itself to us merely as an enigmatic riddle which we are required to understand, but as the demand for faith and obedience. The cross is not just some sort of dialectical puzzle given in order to occupy theologians in their spare time, but discloses the shape and form of Christian existence. Understanding and obedience, theology and ethics, are the proper response to the self-disclosure of God in the crucified Christ. It makes demands of both our hearts and our minds, and is a summons into the real and tangible world of human life and action as much as it is into the world of ideas.

Faith and experience

Christian faith is grounded in, but not controlled by, experience. For Luther, experience had to be interpreted in the light of the paschal mystery, the death and resurrection of Jesus Christ, if it were not to tyrannise the individual believer with his doubts and hopelessness. The paradigm, or model, given to Christians by which they must interpret the experience of their Christian existence is the real experienced bleakness of the cross, interpreted from the standpoint of the resurrection. In the cross of Jesus Christ experience discerns the triumph of death and the forces of might – and at best the wrath, and more likely the total absence of God.

Many of us will have seen John Ford's classic motion picture *Stagecoach*, with its marvellous character studies, and will remember particularly vividly the final part of the action. The stagecoach is being pursued by Indians, who are closing in, and the increasingly desperate occupants of the coach realise that they probably only have a few more minutes to live. Rather than allow some of their number to fall alive into the hands of their pursuers, they save their last bullets for themselves. Then a new element is introduced into the situation, as a bugle call is heard and the US Cavalry appears on the scene to rescue them from their predicament.

No such thing happened on the first Good Friday, although it is evident that many expected that it would. God was perceived to be absent from Calvary: the armies of angels, unlike the US Cavalry in Hollywood westerns, never arrived to rescue their Lord. It is in this night of questioning, doubt and bewilderment, that Christian faith must learn to exist. God raised up Jesus Christ from the dead, but did not deliver him from death itself. The distinctive pattern which is disclosed by the resurrection of the one who was crucified is that of new life being given *through* death, not life being preserved *from* death. But the experience of the absence of God from the first Good Friday – which would be transformed by the events of the first Easter Day – establishes a pattern of divine activity which governs our understanding of the way in which God is present and active in his world.

The experience of Good Friday is real, not illusory: it is only when this real experience is viewed in the light of the resurrection that the strange and mysterious manner in which God was at work can be discerned. The fundamental question raised by Good Friday is that raised earlier, and with such passion, by the book of Job in the Old Testament – Is God *really there*, amidst the contradictions of human experience? The resurrection speaks to us, as from a whirlwind, of the real and redeeming presence of God in situations from which he appears to be absent. Christian existence is life under the cross, life spent in its shadow while we await the dawn of the resurrection light. Christian faith begins where atheism supposes that it must be at an end – with the death of Jesus Christ.

The pastoral implications of these insights will be obvious. The 'theologians of glory' – Luther's scathing term for those who base their thinking about God on something other than the cross – expect God to be experienced as present throughout his creation, and thus find themselves seriously embarrassed by those parts of his creation in which he appears to be conspicuously absent. Where is God in the helplessness of the child dying in great pain from cancer? Such questions must be asked in the face of the dreadful naivete of those who make God's presence conditional upon positive emotional or aesthetic responses to experience. The hand of God may indeed be seen in these experiences – of that there is no dispute. And no one will dispute that the real presence of God becomes almost tangible at points in human experience, when responding to the glories of creation or of human artistic genius. The crux of the problem lies in the inference which is to be drawn from this tendency to make God's presence conditional upon a positive subjective emotional or aesthetic response – that God is not to be found in the more repulsive, distasteful and shocking areas of life. Yet it is in precisely such an area that the Christian tradition claims that the definitive self-revelation of God took place.

The picture of God that is given to us by the cross is that of a deserted, bruised, bleeding and dying God, who lent new meaning and dignity to human suffering by passing through its shadow himself. God enters the world at the very point at which humanity is weak rather than strong, put to shame rather than proud. The darker and inevitable moments of life, culminating in pain, the knowledge of dying and death, are not areas of life from which God has been excluded, but areas in which he has deliberately included himself. God himself chose this way – the way of dereliction and death – to redeem us from these, our last enemies. 'After Good Friday, humanity began to suffer in hope' (Leon Bloy). The powerful image of a God who knows what human suffering and pain are like, who *understands* at first hand what it is like to be weak, frail and mortal, is authorised by the cross of Jesus Christ.

How are we to live knowing that we die? The challenge to human significance posed by the fact that man must die has plagued his efforts at understanding himself down the ages. Death threatens to rob us of meaning. The problem of suffering and evil, culminating in the ultimate threat of human extinction, seems to render invalid from the outset any account of the meaning of human life which is simultaneously *optimistic* and *realistic*. The cynical realist capitulates to what he regards as the facts of the situation in the name of intellectual honesty: 'Eat and drink, for tomorrow we die.' More commonly, both religious and secular ideologies attempt to deny there is a problem, offering a triumphal world-view at the expense of honesty about the way the world really is, perpetrating an illusion of immortality and a utopian conception of human nature and destiny. The cross, seen from the standpoint of the resurrection, allows the believer crucial insights into this dilemma: he knows that life comes through death, not despite it; that Christian hope is born 'on the far side of despair' (John Keats); that the immortal God entered into the mortal situation in order to illuminate it and redeem it.

The threat of death exerts so pervasive an influence over human existence that no philosophy, no religion, no understanding of the world which fails to address it directly can be taken seriously. The denial of death and the threat that it poses to our existence, relevance and meaning is characteristic of the superficial attitude to reality of modern humanity. Yet we must learn to face the fact that we, the greatest of

God's works under the sun, are born only to die. We rise in order to fall, part of the long procession of those who called the world their own, and have now disappeared utterly. We may live on in our children or in the memories of others, but we ourselves cease to exist. Like a bubble that bursts when at its greatest, we pass into the dust of death. Or do we? The crucifixion and resurrection of Jesus Christ firmly anchors eternity in temporality, eternal life in human history, resurrection in death. It is here, in the midst of this world of death and decay, that we catch a glimpse of the far country where our destiny lies, and hear the distant echo of its music.

Perhaps the most difficult and most important test which any ideology (whether religious or secular) can ever face is how it copes with the negative side of life – with despair, with hopelessness, with the growing awareness of the process of dying and the event of death. Perhaps these can be ignored; perhaps they can be denied – but to look them in the face, and know that it is by passing through them, as Christ did before us, that we gain life in its fullness, is the mark of the theology of the cross. 'Socrates mastered the art of dying – Christ overcame death' (Dietrich Bonhoeffer). Favoured with the vantage point of the resurrection of the one who was crucified, the believer is enabled to contemplate failure, suffering and death without either accepting them fatalistically or being reduced to despair by their prospect. God has walked this way before us, exposing the pretensions of experience to finality, and allowing us to see beyond experience to the reality lying behind it. Experience cannot be allowed to have the final word – it must be judged and shown up as deceptive and misleading. The theology of the cross draws our attention to the sheer unreliability of experience as a guide to the presence and activity of God. God is active and present in his world, quite independently of whether we experience him as being so. Experience declared that God was absent from Calvary, only to have its verdict humiliatingly overturned on the third day. The theology of the cross is a theology which is both rooted in and critical of human experience, capable of identifying with it without being trapped or limited by it. This theology interprets, illuminates and transforms human experience, without being reduced to its level.

The 'theology of the cross' deliberately directs the gaze of believers away from their experiences of the risen Christ and the Holy Spirit back to the earthly reality of the cross and the radical demands of faith. Valid and real though these experiences may be, they are a 'foretaste of heaven' (Charles Wesley) rather than a substitute for serious, deliberate and critical engagement with actualising the demands of obedience to God and his gospel on earth. The cross provides the only meaningful barrier to the total detachment of Christians from this life, as they contemplate and rejoice in the hope of eternal life which is theirs through the resurrection of their Lord. It takes this hope, and redirects it, preventing it from becoming unworldly or other-worldly; it directs it towards the transformation of this life in the light of this real and inalienable hope. It is this hope which sustains Christian social and political action – not some oppressive and unacknowledged secular ideology – and without this hope, the vision of the New Jerusalem passes silently into the dust.

The experience of the absence of God

There are points in the believer's life when God seems far away and faith seems to exist in a dark night. Faith may doubt God's existence, his goodness and his love, and the believer may feel himself overwhelmed with existential anxiety. Is God really there? Does God really care for us? Does not death, as the end of all things, make our pathetically short existence devoid of any meaning or significance? Most believers experience feelings such as these at some point in their lives. Like Thomas (John 20:24–29), we may be prepared to admit to our doubts, although many prefer to keep them unknown save to themselves and God. We become aware of a real and confusing contradiction within experience: at times, God's presence and goodness seems to be declared by all of nature, exulting in the knowledge of its creator (Psalm 19:1–4); at other times, the bleakness of human oppression and injustice seems to cry out against the existence and goodness of God.

It is perhaps at moments such as these that faith is forced back to the naked cross, to reflect on what happened as faith was born. On the first Good Friday, God seemed to be absent from his world; he appeared to abandon his chosen Messiah to suffering and death on the cross; he did not intervene to rescue him from his executioners. With the death of Jesus Christ, the seal appeared to have been attached to the death certificate of God: God was not there, and God did not intervene. Good Friday was the darkest night which faith has ever known – and yet, it was during that night that faith was born. For, with the benefit of hindsight, the first Christians realised that God was not absent from that scene of dereliction, but was present as its chief actor. The passion of Jesus Christ was none other than the passion of our God.

As Good Friday gave way to Easter Day, the experience of the absence of God began to assume a new significance. Where was God? And as those bystanders watching Christ die gazed around, looking up to the heavens for deliverance, they saw no sign of God and concluded he was absent. Yet God was there in the event of Calvary, at the one point where none seemed prepared to find him – in the suffering and dying Christ. The presence of God was missed, was overlooked, was ignored, because God chose to be present where none expected to find him – in the suffering, shame, humility, powerlessness and folly of the cross of Jesus Christ. 'God allowed himself to be forced out of the world onto the cross' (Dietrich Bonhoeffer) – God's presence was concentrated and focused on the cross of Jesus Christ. God was absent because he was not present in the way he was expected to be. 'God chose what is foolish in the world to shame the wise, God chose what is weak in the world to shame the strong, God chose what is low and despised in the world' (1 Corinthians 1:27–28 RSV). As if the paradox that 'the Word became flesh' (John 1:14) were not great enough, we have to reckon with the disconcerting fact that the Word was made *broken* flesh.

We can take this point further. The Christian is expected to share in the cross of Christ, bearing the sufferings and ultimately the death which he once bore. But in one important respect the Christian experience of the cross is transformed by the crucifixion and resurrection of Jesus Christ. We can view the cross from the standpoint of the resurrection, which allows us to see the bleakness of that cross in the aura of the resurrection. In this important way the cross of Jesus Christ is not identical with our cross – the resurrection transforms the experiences through which Christians share in the cross of Christ. We need not echo Christ's dreadful cry of God-forsakenness, 'My God, my God, why have you forsaken me?' – because the resurrection allows us to interpret the cross in terms of the hidden presence and victory of God. In this sense we could say that Christ's death upon the cross is substitutionary, in that he bore something in order that we might not bear it. After the resurrection the cross was seen in a very different light – a light in which we now see it. But Jesus Christ experienced the cross in all its bleakness and despair – he experienced as sheer 'cross' what we now experience as 'cross leading to resurrection'. Christ drew the sting of despair and hopelessness from the inevitable end of human life and Christian existence – suffering and death – so that those who travelled the same road after him might contemplate it in a new light.

It is this model which we are given, and expected to use, as we attempt to discern the way in which God is present and active in his world, in his church and in the existence of the individual believer. At times the believer is forced back to the cross itself, in moments of doubt or despair, stripped of all his assurance and anxious to relearn the all too easily forgotten lessons of Calvary. The believer must learn to read the story of the first Good Friday into the story of his present situation – a story of the perceived absence of God, of the despair and dejection of faith when what all thought ought to have happened did not happen. That story was

transformed by the resurrection, the decisive and un-
expected intervention of God, overturning and overwhelming the judgment of the world. God was present –
but not where he was expected. Does God seem to be
absent in our experience? But how unreliable and seductive
a guide to reality experience is! Or, learning of the ruthless
and oppressive suffering of individuals at the hands of their
fellows, we might vent our anger against God, who permits
but does not share such suffering. But our faith, we then
remember, was born as God was condemned by God's
people under God's law and crucified before a taunting
crowd. God has been through the darkest moments of
human existence, taking them up into his history and his
being, and lending them his dignity.

Bearing the cross

The cross stands as the final contradiction of those who
proclaim that becoming a Christian involves an easy
passage through life. In the midst of the euphoria
surrounding the resurrection of Jesus, there was a real
danger that Christian faith and existence would ascend to
the heavens, finally abandoning any point of contact with
the realities of this world. The New Testament, however,
while not attempting to minimise the enormous attraction
and significance of the resurrection of Christ for believers,
deliberately directs attention back to the cross. This tendency is especially evident in the synoptic gospels which –
perhaps with excessive concentration upon the resurrection and a future face-to-face encounter with God in mind –
deliberately direct the attention of believers away from their
experiences of the risen Christ to the demands which their
faith makes upon them here and now. The cross is firmly
and immovably anchored in the midst of human history
and experience, as must the life of the believer also be.
Christian believers exist under the shadow of the cross. The
call to follow Jesus is a call to share in his sufferings (Mark
8:31–38), as well as in his risen glory. The pattern which

believers learn to impose upon their existence is that of journeying *through* suffering, rejection and death *to* eternal life and the glory of the risen Christ. There is no manner in which these may be by-passed. They are the authentic marks of Christian discipleship.

These insights give added weight to the theology of the cross as it bears upon the experience of the individual believer. Suffering, humiliation and rejection are, in effect, the hallmarks of faith, the demonstration that believers are true disciples, the guarantee that they will share in the glory of the risen Christ. Just as believers are baptised with the sign of the cross, to signify that they are children of God, so the life of every child of God is shaped and influenced by the suffering and cross of Jesus Christ. Baptism does not merely stand at the beginning of the Christian life – it symbolises the whole of that life, a constant dying and rising with Christ. By recognising the pattern of the cross – through suffering to glory – in their own experience, believers know that they stand within the promises of God, that they are sharing in the paschal mystery, that they are heirs to the riches of Christ. It is for this reason that Luther emphasises, perhaps to the astonishment of his contemporaries, the positive aspect of suffering. The following passage has already been cited, but is so characteristic that it merits further reflection:

> A theologian of the cross (that is, someone who speaks of the crucified and hidden God) teaches that suffering, the cross and death are the most precious treasure of all, and the most sacred relics which the Lord of this theology has himself consecrated and blessed, not just by the touch of his most holy flesh, but also by the embrace of his most holy and divine will. And he has left these relics here to be kissed, sought after, and embraced. How fortunate and blessed is anyone who is considered by God to be so worthy that these treasures of Christ should be given to him!

Suffering and faith belong together and are directly related in their intensity and quality.

For Luther, the believer and Christ are united in a close union by faith, the believer sharing in the life of Christ, and Christ in the life of the believer. The life of Christ breaks through into that of the believer – what is his, is also ours. And the riches, the heritage, which Christ bestows upon us is the privilege of suffering with him, in order that we may be raised with him; of treading the same path as he once trod, leading first to the cross, and then to glory. It is here that faith is put to the test: does glory really lie beyond the cross? does the cross mark the end of human life, or the beginning of life? The life of faith is a life lived in the firm and steadfast conviction that the cross is the only gate to glory, that it is the only entrance to the New Jerusalem, and that the suffering, pain and contradictions of our life as believers will be resolved and transformed, just as Good Friday gave way to Easter Day. Without the resurrection, the way of the cross is nothing more than ascetic self-denial, at best a way of resignation to the futility of existence, at worst a way of despair and delusion. It is faith in the resurrection of Jesus Christ, and the recognition of its implications for our own existence, which gives the theology of the cross its sense of realism and purpose. To walk on this road is to walk the way of suffering, pain and rejection which leads only to the cross – but faith recognises that we pass through the cross to greet the one who has already passed through it before us, and awaits us on the other side.

'We must respond to Christ's passion, not with words or forms, but with life and truth' (Luther). The cross is not merely the source of ideas about God, but the basis of Christian existence. It stamps the form of the believer's existence and establishes the cross as the natural pattern of Christian life. This idea is far removed from the notion that 'bearing our cross' is some form of meritorious work, which only the more spiritually enlightened believer need under-take. Precisely because the believer shares in Christ's passion, his existence is shaped by the cross. We could say that the cross of Christ is taken up in an existential manner by the believer. Anything which serves to detach the believer from the cross – whether material riches or spiritual pride – is a potential threat to the vitality and authenticity of his Christian life. 'The cross of Christ is nothing else than forsaking everything and clinging with the heart's faith to Christ alone' (Luther). The cross, with all that this entails, is laid upon the believer as part of his Christian life – and in recognising and accepting this fact the believer clinches his calling. He does not need to seek the cross for he already stands under it. It is not something chosen by the believer – it is something which is imposed upon him through that very faith. The spiritual growth of the believer is largely concerned with the increasing recognition that his entire life is inextricably linked with the passion, death and resurrection of Jesus Christ, and thus *becoming* what he *already is*: 'The real and true work of the passion of Christ is to conform us to Christ' (Luther).

The cross and the values of the believer

The greatest obstacle that we may place in the path of God is our self. And that obstacle must be eliminated if we are to be reforged and refashioned after the manner of the crucified Christ. 'It is necessary that we should be destroyed and rendered formless, in order that Christ may be formed and may be alone within us' (Luther). The cross breaks down our spiritual, intellectual and moral pride, disclosing to us how empty and vain they really are. The natural human tendency to regard ourselves as spiritually, morally and intellectually autonomous prevents us from looking outside of ourselves, in order to find the help we need. Luther suggested that 'man is curved in on himself' (*incurvatus in se*), in a form of spiritual narcissism. Humanity is simply unaware of the inadequacy of its own soteriological resources, of the cruel fact that it cannot save itself. We find it difficult to understand that the faculties which we prize so highly – our reason, our religious inclinations, and so on – are actually obstacles to God, rather than grounds on which

LIFE UNDER THE CROSS: THE CHURCH

Testament, the church – the community of
en called out from the world by the cross and
f Jesus Christ in order to be sent back into it
hem. So intimate is the New Testament
e Pauline) understanding of the connection
urch and the crucified and risen Christ that
t be recognised as the 'body of Christ' (1
6; 12:13). The body of Christ dying upon
ised from the dead has been transposed
d with, the body of Christ on earth – the
th, the Christian church. But what is the
What has it been called into existence to
ay be used to determine whether or not
observe in western society really are
The questions raised by Martin Luther
rs of the sixteenth century retain their
: Is the church faithful to its calling?
ing to recall it to faithfulness, and at

ety-Five Theses on the door of the
nberg in 1517 Luther brought into
e now call the Reformation, which
shattering the unity of the western
urch to its true mission and calling.
costly business – which is why the
uate and judge itself *continually*, in
The church must be *ecclesia semper*
ich is continually open to self-
great events which brought her

God may build. For this reason God must destroy before he can build.

The basic problem is not so much that our basic and natural human insights concerning righteousness, spirituality, personal holiness, and so on, are wrong: this is far from being the case; in fact they often serve as points of contact between God and humanity, bridgeheads by which revelation may be interpreted and understood. The problem arises through our reluctance to look beyond ourselves, to admit that help is needed if our situation is to be transformed, to concede our personal inadequacies. In short, our self-confidence must be shattered so that amidst the wreckage of our self-esteem we may discover the means by which we may rebuild our understanding of God and ourselves. The cross forces us to a point where we concede our inadequacies and turn instead to God.

Jesus Christ was crucified by people who were moral, religious and conscientious – people who are uncomfortably like ourselves. We miss the central point of the narrative of the crucifixion if we imagine that those who were responsible for the crucifixion of Jesus were any less moral, religious or conscientious than we ourselves are. The Messiah was killed by God's own people under God's own law. Even our best-informed moral, religious and spiritual insights can be seriously perverted to the point where they prevent us from finding God, even when he is present in the midst of us.

Our moral and religious insights are all too often like Towers of Babel, human structures defiantly erected in the face of God. We have created them, perhaps unconsciously – and we have not been authorised to do so. Our insights derive from many sources, and are generally uncritically synthesised into an outlook on life which owes little to God. The cross passes judgment upon these Towers of Babel, sweeping them away as mere fiction, and confronting us with a vision of the living God. Far from endorsing our natural insights, God contradicts them – not necessarily because they are wrong, but because they have been erected into a defensive wall which excludes God. The cross represents an act of God which is simultaneously annihilating and creative – it destroys our preconceptions of God, and in their place allows the living God to make his entrance. The cross places a question mark against our values, and directs our gaze away from ourselves, towards God. It assists us to remove the obstacle which we ourselves place in God's way.

Throughout its history humanity has demonstrated a consistent tendency to move from the creature to the creator, preferring to overlook what Kierkegaard called the 'infinite qualitative distinction' between God and humanity. Humanity expects God to endorse its moral and religious insights – whereas they are instead shattered and exposed for the inadequate caricatures which they are, through the self-revelation of God in Jesus Christ. To take the cross seriously is to recognise that theology is about the movement of God towards us, focused upon the figure of Jesus Christ as he is nailed to the cross. Our efforts to comprehend God must give way to God's self-disclosure of himself as he would have us know him – in the crucified Christ. The cross 'breaks down all righteousness and wisdom of our own' (Luther), reminding us that God is, and always will be, none other than the living God, uncontrollable by either theological faculties or synods of bishops. It invites us to set aside our preconceptions of what God must be like, and on what terms he may be encountered, in order to meet him at Calvary. We are forced to rediscover the deity of God and the sheer inadequacy of our attempts to portray him.

It is for this reason that the theology of the cross is a theology of humility – a willingness to see things as they really are, reflected in the cross. In the words of T. S. Eliot:

> The only wisdom we can hope to acquire
> Is the wisdom of humility. Humility is endless.
>
> *East Coker*

A penetrating and disturbing challenge to our perceptions – indeed, to our *preconceptions* – of 'truth' and 'reality' is

8

addressed to us, as the theology
names things for what they rea
to act upon these insights. Th
of humility which must shap
believer as he stands under i
our self-confidence and cor
tion that the illusion has t
reality may be built. The cr
tion; but in that it expose
and morality, and forces
in reality spells forgive
grace won at a cost. Th
our self-assurance, b
inadequacies. It is
sufficiency of the b
to recognise tha
strength lie not
but in the God
cross.

For the Ne
faith – has b
resurrection
to proclaim
(particularly t
between the ch
the church mu
Corinthians 10
the cross and r
into, or identifie
community of fa
church there for?
do? What criteria r
the institutions w
Christian churches
and the other reform
relevance even toda
And if not, who is g
what cost?
By posting his Nir
castle church at Witt
being the movement v
tried – at the expense o
church – to recall the ch
Reformation imposed is a
church must learn to eval
the light of its title deeds.
reformanda, the church w
correction in the light of th

into being and called her out of the world in order to serve the world. The Christian church must recognise that it stands *today* before that same Wittenberg door, to read the truth by which she was called into existence and by which she is judged.

The mission of the church

The Christian church came into being as a response to the event of the crucifixion and resurrection of Jesus Christ. No other reason for its origins may be convincingly given. She was called out of the world in order to be sent back into the world with the gospel proclamation. The need to distinguish the Christian community from the Jewish context within which it had its origins arose through the scandal of the cross – the proclamation that Jesus Christ, the long-awaited Messiah had been crucified and raised from the dead by God (e.g., see Acts 2:22–36; 1 Corinthians 1:22–23). It was on the basis of the proclamation of the resurrection of the crucified Christ that the church expanded into the Mediterranean world, breaking free from the cultural strait-jacket of first-century Judaism. 'We preach Christ crucified' (1 Corinthians 1:23) – this was the manifesto of the Christian church at a point in its history when it was confident of its reason for existence and relevance for mankind. Both the identity and the mission of the Christian church were originally unequivocally and inextricably linked with the proclamation of the resurrection of the crucified Christ.

Is there any reason why this situation should have changed? In the first period of its existence the church exulted in the fact that it had been *given* its reason for existence, the basis of its identity and relevance – it did not have to *seek* a role through which it could justify its existence to the world. It had been given its role as the bearer and proclaimer of the good news of the resurrection of the crucified Jesus Christ and of the implications of this astonishing event for the world. No other body had this role. If this good news was found to be wrong, inadequate or irrelevant, the existence of the church into the second century and beyond would have been improbable, to say the least. And so the church was forced to put all its eggs in one basket, so to speak: it took its stand against the world on the basis of its proclamation that Christ, who had been crucified, really had been raised from the dead, and that the ramifications of this event extended far and wide in time and space. The identity and relevance, and hence the existence, of the church would stand or fall with the truth of this remarkable assertion.

As time went on the church became established within the Roman Empire through the conversion of Constantine, and subsequently throughout much of Europe until the rise of the Enlightenment in the eighteenth century. The church acquired new roles within society, such as that of the guardian of morality. The church became consolidated within western society and assimilated to its structures and values. Although western society continues to allow the church to perform certain limited social roles, it is increasingly clear that these are in the process of being usurped or reclaimed by secular agencies. This is not to say that, for example, because social service agencies care for the poor, the church may cease to do so – but it is to say that the church can no longer think of itself as being *defined* by this role. The roles imposed upon the church by society, or claimed by the church for herself within society, are in the process of being withdrawn. Is it not time for the church to reclaim the one role which is hers and hers alone? Is it not time for the church to recall the days of her youth, when faith was young and vibrant, and when she was confident that she had something important and relevant to say to the world? The changing face of western society, particularly the withdrawal from the church of many of the roles it had once been allocated within that society, has been – and ought to be! – the occasion of a serious identity crisis within the western churches, forcing them to ask why they exist at all. If the church merely performs roles which others perform (and perform more professionally), it has no business to continue in existence. There is no sadder sight than a church which has lost the social roles which it chose and is unwilling to assume the role which was originally given to it, to which the New Testament eloquently witnesses: 'Go . . . and make disciples of all nations' (Matthew 28:19).

The fact is that the church was given, and still possesses, a distinctive role – a role given to her as her birthright, and which she has all too often tended to treat as Esau treated his birthright: something which, because it was neither tangible nor material, could be traded in for some pottage (Genesis 25:29–34). The material benefits of this trade-in may have satisfied some temporary need at the time, but in the long term it must be recognised as an act of remarkable folly. It is time to reclaim that birthright, and with it the church's claim to both identity and relevance. This suggestion may be viewed as an act of regression, contrary to our ideas of progress. How can we turn the clock back? Is not the way ahead to be gained by going forward, rather than backward? But when a road seems to lead nowhere, despite its promising beginnings, it is time to turn back, retracing our steps, in order to find where we went wrong – and then to try once more to find the right road. Progress is not made by doggedly pursuing our present course of action, but by critically evaluating our position and making any adjustments necessary – including the undoing of what has already been done. To keep going in the same road is the mark of theological conservatism, not progressiveness. To return to the cross is to swim against the currents and views dominating certain types of western Christianity – but to swim against the current is to find and reach its source, which is, as it always has been (whether acknowledged or not) the cross and resurrection of Jesus Christ.

In all the discussions concerning the relevance of the church to modern society, or ecumenical discussions concerning the *esse* ('essential nature') and *bene esse* ('wellbeing') of the church, there appears to have been a remarkable reluctance to recognise that a church which has ceased to have a mission has not merely ceased to be relevant – it has ceased to be the Christian church. The church does not exist for its own sake, but for the sake of both the one who died in order that she might have a gospel to proclaim and of those who wish to hear that gospel. To fail in the task of the proclamation of the resurrection of the crucified Christ, and the impact and relevance of this event for the human situation, is to forfeit both the *bene esse* and the *esse* of the church. Mission does indeed involve responsible social action and involvement – but the 'word of the cross' remains a *word*, something which must be heard and understood, something which must be proclaimed in order to find a response.

The call of the church to mission is thus a catalyst, a stimulus, to the process of grounding the theology and the proclamation of that church in human reality. The church must reaffirm her being and existence by living in mission, conscious of the seriousness and urgency of her task to both her own future wellbeing, and also of her responsibility to the God who called her into existence in the first place. The growing indifference or hostility towards academic theology within the western church is ultimately grounded in the suspicion that this theology has become trapped in the upper regions of the towers of academia and requires to be brought down to the ground floor of human reality if it is to regain its purpose and relevance. Mission and theology are so closely interrelated that they cannot be permitted to become divorced in the manner to which western academic theologians have become accustomed. After all, in Jesus Christ God himself came down to earth, down to the level of us mortals, and it ought not to be beyond the capacities of theologians to do the same.

Theology must come down to earth, to serve the church and its mission to the world – and if it will not come down to earth, it must be *brought* down to earth by so marginalising academic theology within the life of the church that it ceases to have any relevance to that church, in order that a theology orientated towards the pastoral and missiological needs of the church may develop in its wake. Academic theology, by demanding the right to set its own agenda and employ its own methods, has increasingly distanced itself from the life and concerns of the Christian church and can therefore have little cause for complaint if it finds itself increasingly marginalised by that church. Theology must be orientated towards the life of the church if it is to have any relevance to that life. All too often academic theologians seem to imagine themselves as determining the great and ultimate questions upon which the existence of God and the life of the church depend, with all and sundry awaiting the outcome of their debate with bated breath – whereas they may more realistically be compared with ducks fighting over some scraps of bread in a pond, engaged in their own private and limited squabbles while the world passes them by on its business. And here the 'theology of the cross' assumes its foundational and critical role, by inviting us to return to the point from which the mission of the church began, both historically and theologically, in the resurrection of the one who was crucified, in order that we may regain a sense of perspective and a sense of *excitement*, of having something powerful and exhilarating to say, as we return to face the world in our own day and age.

Triumphalism within the church

To return to the cross is to view the problems facing the Christian church from the standpoint of the event which brought the church into being, which shapes its outlook on the world and governs its thinking about its identity and relevance. For Luther, the 'theologian of the cross' is to be contrasted with the 'theologian of glory' – perhaps the latter phrase is best translated into modern English as 'triumphalist'. The theology of the cross is a critical theology, and that criticism is not directed primarily against the world, but against certain triumphalist trends within Christianity itself. Before the church can criticise the world she must first be self-critical. (This is not to say that the theology of the cross is a *negative* theology, although there are some parallels with what is known as the 'apophatic' or 'negative' approach to theology.) There is a tendency in some quarters of the church to suggest that the resurrection of Jesus *supersedes* the cross – in other words, that the Christian life ought to be lived in the power of the resurrection rather than under the shadow of the cross. Through faith, it can be argued, we may appropriate and make our own the power of the resurrection here and now. The church ought to live in the light and power of the resurrection.

The force of this point is obvious. Without the resurrection the Christian faith makes no sense at all. The death of Christ would have been a catastrophe, putting an end to any form of Christianity other than the perpetuation of a rabbi's teaching within the Jewish tradition. Attempts to 'water down' the resurrection (for example, by restating it in terms of the survival of the memory of Jesus, instead of a historical event) carry little conviction – they may be easy to believe, but they are hardly worth believing. The idea that the resurrection of Jesus was a purely 'spiritual' affair, while his corpse remained in the tomb, is a rather modern idea, apparently resting upon the somewhat dogmatic view of reality held by the thinkers of the Enlightenment. The reality of the resurrection, both as a historical event and a personal experience, dominates early Christian preaching, just as it dominates the Christian tradition which derives from it. But the profundity, the full force, of the triumph of the resurrection can only be appreciated in the light of the crucifixion, which defines the 'before' to which the resurrection is the 'after'. To play down the significance of the crucifixion is to cheapen the triumph of the resurrection.

More importantly, the call to follow Jesus is a call to participate in his suffering, rejection and cross *before* his resurrection. The way of faith leads through the cross to the resurrection. The Christian church is the people of God on earth, perhaps with one foot already firmly planted on the other side of the cross, perhaps with a real experience of the power of the resurrection here and now – but, at best, this power breaks through into a world dominated by the bleakness of the cross. The cross remains the fundamental statement concerning the human situation and God's manner of dealing with it. The church must learn to conquer in weakness, as Christ did. It may, at times, be difficult for a church which has tasted the resurrection life to root itself in the world and address itself to the present situation. But just as Christ addressed the world from the pulpit of his cross, the church must learn that it is this cross – viewed in the light of the resurrection, to be sure – which is *authorised* as the basis of the Christian proclamation. 'I decided to know nothing among you except Jesus Christ and him crucified' (1 Corinthians 2:2 RSV). The cross demonstrates the totality of God's engagement with the forces of evil and darkness which dominate the world – and the church must make that engagement its own, taking it with equal serious- ness and basing it upon that same cross. The cross marks God's decisive participation in human history – the parti- cipation of a suffering and redeeming love which alters the world, not through dictating its course from outside, but by altering it from within, through solidarity with suffering humanity. God enters the stream of human history, rides it as its flood and alters its course.

The Christian church, being human, has found the 'word of the cross' a serious embarrassment at points. Those who tread the ecclesiastical corridors of power find themselves challenged by the cross: God works through the powerless, and continually threatens to contradict those who wish to work otherwise, such as by modelling the church upon secular institutions of power. While it is clearly impossible for the church to return to a pre-Constantinian innocence in which it renounces any interest in the realities of political power, it is imperative that the church bases her under- standing of the manner in which power is to be exercised upon a God-given, rather than a secular, model. The human instinct to gain and exercise power is contradicted by the cross, which demonstrates that the exercise of power within the church is a jealously guarded divine prerogative that is not to be usurped. Perhaps one of the most telling arguments for original sin is the continual struggle for power within the hierarchies or committees of the church – the one community which ought to know better. If salva- tion is merely concerned with education, as some suggest,

the apparent inability of at least some sections of the
Christian church to learn from the example of Christ must
call into question whether salvation thus understood really
is a genuine possibility.

The Christian church presents an all too human face to
the world. The power struggles of ecclesiastical committees; the contempt with which many academic theologians
treat the 'humble believer'; the quest for recognition and
relevance of the clergy in the eyes of the world: in all these
matters, and countless others, the church betrays how
profoundly human an organisation it really is. And even
the most sympathetic of its observers will be justified in
asking a simple and penetrating question: What has an
organisation like this got to do with a man dying upon a
cross? Is *this* why he died? There is a need for both the
churchman and the theologian to be forced to return to
Calvary, to the event upon which their faith and their
present occupations are based. Their perspective upon life
and their calling might be improved by rubbing their collective noses in the blood and gore of that cross, in order to
remind them of the full seriousness and cost of the redemption of humanity, with whose proclamation they are
entrusted. The scene of divine humility, of *humiliation*, at
Calvary is profoundly threatening – it threatens to contradict both the lifestyle and the theological presuppositions of
the community whose faith is based upon it. And, as the
history of the church demonstrates, reform from within the
church is greatly to be preferred to reform which is imposed
upon a church from outside. But, as Luther himself knew, a
church which will not reform itself in accordance with the
model given in the crucified Christ must – despite the
appalling consequences – be called to account in other
ways. The cross is the foundation and the criterion of
both the Christian church and Christian theology – and the
dual nature of its function means that its influence upon
that church and that theology is both threatening and
disturbing.

Perhaps one of the finest religious poems ever written is
the eighth-century Anglo-Saxon *Dream of the Rood*. In this

poem, the writer (whose identity remains a mystery) tells of how he dreamt a dream, the 'best of dreams', in which he saw a cross covered with gold and studded with precious stones, shining brilliantly in all its glory. The reference is almost certainly to the glorious jewelled crosses carried in triumph through the churches of the time during the great festivals. But then, as the poet looks upon the cross, it changes its appearance before his eyes, and gold and jewels give way to blood and gore, as the full horror of the original scene of crucifixion is brought before him. The triumphalism of the processional cross is contrasted with an uncompromisingly explicit description of the grim and gruesome process of crucifixion. The tree is 'pierced with dark nails' and 'made wet all over with blood' – and these ornaments and this covering are contrasted with the jewels and gold with which the triumphal cross was decorated.

Inevitably, the poem forces us to recall that behind the triumph of the celebrations of the church lies a deeply disturbing and distressing scene, as the salvation of the world was won through blood and nails. We are forced to ask what the connection is between the pomp and triumph of the church and the event upon which that church is founded. Here, as elsewhere, we must continually ask, 'What has *this* to do with Jesus Christ dying upon a cross?' Just as the poet's vision oscillated in a creative and insightful tension between gold and blood, jewels and nails, so we must temper and criticise our natural tendency to triumphalism in the light of the contradiction of that tendency in the cross of Jesus Christ.

The theology of the cross identifies the intimate relation between faith, obedience and suffering, and asserts that the greatest treasure bequeathed to his church by her Lord is the privilege of sharing in those sufferings. Christ's obedience and sufferings are those of his body, the church, which must bear the marks of his nails in her flesh.

The cross reminds the Christian church that there is simply no room for complacency, self-confidence or triumphalism within its bounds. The church has a mission – a mission which it continually demonstrates itself incapable of meeting. Reluctant to concede its failure in its mission, the church tends to yield to the seductive temptation to find alternative, more attractive roles, where success is more tangible, more easily attained and more easily demonstrated to have been attained. Yet the church must not be allowed to delude itself or distract itself in this manner. Just as the church cannot be allowed to say 'Amen!' to every culturally-conditioned social affirmation or expectation, so it must learn that external criteria of relevance imposed upon it by society should give way to its inner criterion of relevance and identity – the cross and resurrection of Jesus Christ.

The church and culture

Modern western society may expect the church to endorse its each and every presupposition, lending it an aura of sanctity and divinity – but the church must learn to distinguish between what society expects of her and what her calling as the church of God demands of her. Western liberal culture has its own gods, which the church must recognise as idols. Just as the Old Testament prophets protested in the name of God against the appropriation of the gods of Canaan by the people of Israel, so the theologian must protest in the name of that same God against the establishment of a pantheon within the church – a pantheon in which the values and expectations of western liberal culture are given equal place with, or identified with, God.

Of all the cultures now known to man it is modern western culture which offers the greatest resistance to the gospel – not least because of the absorption of its values and presuppositions by the Christian church, the very institution which has a mission to challenge them. Time after time the western church demonstrates itself to be the secret prisoner of western culture, trapped within its web, apparently both unable and unwilling to free itself and others through the liberating gospel of redemption in

Christ. For example, there is a reluctance on the part of some western clergy to preach the gospel, on the grounds that it might compromise the integrity of their audience. In effect, this amounts to the admission that within their pantheon, at least one deity – the principle of not compromising cultural integrity – is to be placed higher than God himself.

Examples of the mere endorsement of the values and expectations of contemporary society by the Christian church are legion. Many modern Anglicans, for example, shake their heads in disbelief on reading the famous lines of a former Bishop of London, speaking during the First World War, who declared that God would gratefully receive 'each and every man who died for his country' with the words, 'Well done, thou good and faithful servant.' Yet we so easily lose sight of the fact that, at the time, those words were regarded as proper, both inside and outside the church. Our distress and disbelief at those words ought, however, to be allowed to serve a useful purpose – that of challenging us to ask whether contemporary church leaders are simply following the lead set them by the social and political subculture which they find congenial, rather than attempting to bring authentically Christian insights to bear. Just as that bygone Bishop of London endorsed the established expectations of contemporary British society, others today unconsciously do exactly the same – and just as we, so long afterwards, can see the obvious absurdity and offensiveness of that bishop's remarks, we must remember that others in the future may well pass a similar judgment upon our pronouncements, if we make the same mistake. Conformity to external criteria of relevance may gain some advantage in the short term, but in the long term it is counterproductive. Tactically helpful in the struggle for social recognition, it is strategically of questionable value.

A further point concerns the nature of culture itself. There is a tendency within the western churches to regard western culture as something which is 'given', something which defines the major premise of the theological syllo-

182 THE ENIGMA OF THE CROSS

gism, where the crucified and risen Jesus Christ is but the minor premise. This view would seem to lack both social perceptiveness and theological insight. It is not merely individual human beings who are fallen and trapped in their situations – both human society and particularly western culture are equally fallen and enslaved to sin. The bondage of western culture to market forces and the extent of its manipulation by vested interests at least call into question, and more probably discredit, the suggestion that such a culture is something God-given which must be respected and treated as lying beyond criticism. God is not bound by culture, although he may operate within or in terms of a given cultural situation – and if he is trapped within a culture, or outside a culture, then it is we who have thus trapped him.

God can neither be identified with a culture's values nor can he be set up as the total and absolute contradiction of those values. An uncritically affirmative approach to a culture is just as misguided as its uncritically negative counterpart. In the place of these seductive simplifications, we must learn to wrestle with the awkward fact that God must ultimately be recognised to be above each and every culture, but as employing cultures as the vehicles of his interactions with humanity. The gospel affirms culture as a vehicle of divine revelation, allowing points of contact to be established, while simultaneously criticising it in the light of that revelation. The gospel, by rooting itself in culture, is forced to address the question of its relation to that culture, ultimately to call it into question. Just as God assumed human nature in order to redeem it, so the gospel assumes cultures. And just as the doctrine of the incarnation does not mean that God and humanity can be *identified*, so the cultural contextualisation of the gospel does not imply that 'gospel' and 'culture' are one and the same thing. Thus the gospel, which has always been embodied in human cultures, must ultimately call into question the values and presuppositions of those cultures. The Christian church is thus forced to adopt a critical attitude towards its own cultural context, as well as to those cultural contexts into which it may wish to expand and develop: it can allow itself neither to endorse the values of that culture nor to dismiss them. Instead, a careful process of evaluation must be undertaken, in the light of the criterion which gives and guarantees the identity and relevance of the Christian gospel and church within any cultural situation – the cross of Jesus Christ.

While social criticism remains an important aspect of the witness of the Christian church, however, it cannot be regarded as its primary function. Its central and essential mission remains the same, and is that which was historically given to the community of faith at its birth – the proclamation of the resurrection of the crucified Christ, the 'word of the cross'. The proclamation of the criterion of social criticism must precede that criticism, both logically and theologically. Whatever other interests and preoccupations the church may develop must be recognised as peripheral. It may seem foolish and pointless, in the face of all the concerns of the world, and the church will be perennially tempted to seek relevance in things which seem more important and relevant by the standards of the age. Yet God, in his wisdom, has given the church which dares to call itself the church *of God* the substance of its proclamation and its reason for existence in his world. We may be unable to understand why he should have done this – we may even share the suspicion that it is sheer madness – but the simple, if disconcerting, fact remains that we are simply not *authorised* to substitute anything else as the essential feature of the Christian proclamation. We cannot set ourselves over and against the judgment of the Christian tradition without calling into question our right to call ourselves 'Christian'. We cannot violate the integrity of the Christian tradition: we may adapt it to the situation, contextualising it and establishing points of contact with it, but the 'word of the cross' transcends those situations and cannot be reduced to them or identified with them. The 'word of the cross' is the true treasure of the church, belonging to past and future generations as well as our own. It is something 'given', which we may accept or reject – but to alter it significantly is to step outside the stream of the Christian tradition and found a new religion.

The church and the cross

The Christian church is defined, both historically and theologically, in terms of the aftermath of the crucifixion – reflection upon the meaning of the resurrection of the one who was crucified, and the joyful proclamation of this event and its meaning to the world. In its worship the church joyfully proclaims that she, like her saviour and Lord, dies to rise again. In the sacraments of baptism and the Eucharist the corporate death of the community to sin and its rise to new life is recalled and celebrated, and presented as a real and present possibility for those outside its bounds. It is here that the language game which defines 'salvation' is played. Just as the cross proclaims that eternal life is gained through death, so the bread and wine – the symbols of death – proclaim the new life made available in a world of death through the resurrection of the one who was crucified. A symbol of defeat becomes a symbol of victory. Just as Israel recalled her deliverance from bondage in Egypt through Moses and the exodus (Psalm 105), so the church joyfully declares that she was called into existence through the deliverance from sin and death accomplished through the crucifixion and resurrection of Jesus Christ. It was from here that the Christian church began its mission – and it is to here that the Christian church must return to rediscover, reclaim and regain that mission, in order that she may go forward conquering and to conquer in the sign of strength made perfect in weakness: the cross of Jesus Christ.

The legacy of the dying Christ to his disciples and his church was the cross, the symbol of shame, dereliction and despair turned into astonishment and joy by the resurrection from the dead. The cross was no moral victory which vindicated the integrity of the one who died upon it. Without the resurrection Christianity has nothing to offer the world but some interesting and ultimately sterile ideas.

The reason that these ideas did not find their way into the footnotes of some learned work on first-century Jewish sects was the simple and disconcerting fact that the early Christians knew that their saviour and Lord had been raised from the dead. It was not just that his ideas were vindicated, but that he himself had been raised to glory, propelling his church into the unknown future armed with the knowledge of his continuing redeeming presence (Matthew 28:20). The great Christian themes of hope and joy converge upon the cross of the one who was crucified and raised from the dead. It is through faith in the God who raised Jesus Christ from the dead, who overturned the verdict of the world, that the Christian church must go forward into history, if she is to remain a significant part of that history.

Like a beacon upon a hill the cross stands as a sign of the love and compassion of God, summoning to its feet sinful humanity. The Christian church is the community which gathers at the foot of that cross to wonder and adore the God who is hidden and yet revealed in its shame and suffering, and who makes so powerful and telling an appeal in his powerlessness and weakness. It is here that the true knowledge of God and ourselves is to be had – and that knowledge is deeply wounding to both the believer and the church, in that it exposes both for what they really are: naked, weak, impotent, sinful and foolish. Yet it is through being wounded that we are healed and go forth to heal. It is through recognising our nakedness, weakness, impotence, sinfulness and foolishness that we turn to the God who called the church into being, in order to receive from him healing and wholeness (Revelation 3:17–19) and to offer this healing to others.

The theology of the cross is thus a theology of hope – hope for those who are oppressed by the fear of death, by the seeming meaninglessness of suffering, by the contradictions of Christian experience, by the threat of extinction, by the apparent weakness and foolishness of the Christian gospel. In the tension, the dialectic, between the crucifixion and resurrection lies the key to the Christian understanding of existence, and the recovery of the identity and relevance of the Christian faith and the Christian church. It is a theology of hope for those who despair of the present state of the Christian churches, who wonder how on earth they can even survive, let alone develop.

Yet it is not upon human strength and wisdom that the continued existence of the church depends. The graveyards of the world are full of individuals who believed that the existence and life of the church depended upon them, yet the grave could not hold the one upon whom that existence and life ultimately depend. For the theology of the cross involves the recognition that it is *God's* gospel, revealed and made perfect in what the world regarded as stupidity and weakness. The proclamation of the word of the cross has a power of its own which transcends the weakness and sinfulness of those who proclaim it. The same God who was hidden in the sufferings of the cross is hidden in the weakness of his church, overcoming it and transforming it. Let Luther have the final word to that church:

It is not we who can sustain the church, nor was it those who came before us, nor will it be those who come after us. It was, and is, and will be the one who says 'I am with you always, even to the end of time'. As it says in Hebrews 13: 'Jesus Christ, the same *yesterday*, *today* and *forever*'. And in Revelation 1: 'Who *was*, and *is*, and *is to come*'. Truly, he is that one, and no one else is, or ever can be. For you and I were not alive thousands of years ago, yet the church was sustained without us – and it was done by the one of whom it says: 'Who *was*' and '*Yesterday*' . . . The church would perish before our very eyes, and we along with it (as we demonstrate every day), if it were not for that other man who so obviously upholds the church and us. This we can lay hold of and feel, even if we are reluctant to believe it. We must give ourselves to the one of whom it is said: 'Who *is*' and '*Today*'. Again, we can do nothing to sustain the church when we are dead. But he will do it, of whom it is said: 'Who *is to come*', and '*Forever*'.

CONCLUSION

In this book we have been exploring the centrality and relevance of the cross of Jesus Christ for the Christian faith, the Christian believer and the Christian church, based on the insight that we are *authorised* to speak about God on the basis of the crucified Christ.

All too often the cross is relegated to sections of theological textbooks dealing with 'theories of the atonement' or 'soteriology'. Yet this is unacceptable: the cross is not just about one chapter of the Christian faith; it casts its shadow and stamps its form upon *all* of that theology – and not just *academic* theology, but theology in its proper sense of 'talk about God', embracing every aspect of our existence as Christians. For this reason we have largely avoided discussion of 'theories of the atonement', in order to bring out the importance of the cross for the whole existence, the life and doctrine, of the Christian church.

All too often the cross is treated as something of importance in relation to the initiation or inauguration of the Christian life, but which exercises no subsequent influence over that life. Yet the cross does not merely establish the starting point of the Christian life, it shapes our understanding of its nature and purpose, and the manner in which God is present and active in his world and our lives. To become a Christian is to live under the cross of Jesus Christ and to view God, the world and the life of faith in its light. The cross is the true treasure of the Christian church, entrusted to her in order that she may remain the steward of the mysteries of faith until the end of time.

This book is intended as a catalyst to stimulate the

reader's thinking on the full relevance of the cross to his faith. Just as a jeweller will hold up a cut diamond to a light and rotate it in order that its many facets may be reflected in their full brilliance, we have attempted to explore the many facets of the cross and their relevance to the Christian faith. It is, however, quite simply impossible to do full justice to the themes so tentatively explored in this work. Its all too obvious shortcomings reflect the inadequacies of its author, rather than of its subject, and it is hoped that the reader will find himself sufficiently excited or irritated by it to reflect further on the enigma of the cross.

On the front cover of this work may be found Salvador Dali's *Christ of St John of the Cross*. This painting is a powerful portrayal of the world seen from the standpoint of the cross, in which the cross of Jesus Christ dominates our view of the world. To see the world, to view reality, we must see it from and through the cross. And it is this standpoint which we, as Christians, must learn to assume as we survey the world in which we live. It is from this perspective that we must look at existence. The foreground of our view of reality is dominated by the crucified Christ, just as our perception of what lies beyond is shaped by that same cross. It is this specific historical event, this highly evocative image, which exposes all other theological speculation as mere shadow-boxing which fails to engage with God as he may be found.

The cross remains the annihilating and creative act of God which places our tidy theological systems and our attempts to assimilate religion and culture in the balance and finds them wanting. It is this picture which holds the church and the believer captive and which discloses a pattern of divine activity which governs our outlook upon existence in faith. To be a theologian of the cross is to approach God at the place and in the form in which he has chosen to disclose himself: the dying Christ as he hangs outstretched upon the cross. It is to wrestle with the riddle of that cross, knowing that in doing so we are wrestling with a God who is hidden in its suffering and shame, with a knowledge which will wound us before it heals us. The cross may ultimately defy explanation, but it certainly demands a response.

In the end the cross must remain the enigmatic and deeply disturbing centre of the Christian faith. It remains the opaque window through which we may and must view God and which we can never bypass. Who God is, and what is divine; who we are, and what is human – these cannot be discovered by free enquiry, but only learnt in humility there, where God has chosen to reveal himself. The 'obedience of faith' (Romans 1:5), the demand for understanding and commitment, is grounded in the appeal to us made by the dying Christ from his cross. The beginning and the end of all knowledge of God consists not in a universal and abstract concept of 'divinity', but in the particular figure and historical person of Jesus Christ, as he was crucified. Nor is the cross some form of theological learning aid which the church may dispense with once she has learnt her theology. As Luther reminded us, we must learn to return to that cross, there to learn our theology all over again.

I remember once being at a conference organised by our local English diocese. Part of this conference consisted of an exercise designed to stimulate our powers of reflection. We were all required to sit in a circle and contemplate an object for an hour, and then report our findings to a plenary session. The object we were forced to contemplate was a brick. It was not a particularly inspiring brick. None of us particularly wanted to contemplate the brick either – the beautiful Nottinghamshire countryside was beckoning to us through an open window, and we would all have much rather contemplated that landscape! However, we had little choice in the matter – the conference organisers were present and ensured that we did as we were told!

The Christian church is in a similar position. She might much prefer to contemplate something other than the dying Jesus Christ – but her thoughts about God and the world must be based upon that haunting and deeply disturbing image of the 'crucified and hidden God'. The church is the community drawn out of the world to assemble at the foot of the cross in wonder, worship and adoration. It is this picture which holds her captive. It is this scene which the church commemorates wherever and whenever she meets to adore and worship the God who called her into being. It is this model of power and authority which must govern the relation of believers among themselves and the relation of the church to the world. It is this pattern of life through death, glory through suffering, which illuminates and informs our understanding of Christian existence.

To be a theologian of the cross is to recognise that we are simply not authorised to base responsible Christian discussion of God or ourselves upon anything other than the crucified and risen Christ, and to exult in and wonder at the astonishing and liberating understanding of God which results. Just as two lovers may return to the place at which their love was born, in order to recapture both the memories which that place holds and the original vitality and freshness of that love, so the Christian church must learn to return to the place at which its faith was born, in order to remember the despair of the cross and the joy of the resurrection and recapture once more the sense of wonder and excitement which underlies the Christian faith. And if we have lost that sense of wonder, perhaps it is time to return to that cross, there to learn the story of God's dealings with us all over again.

Like Mary let us ponder in our mind
God's wondrous love in saving lost mankind;
Trace we the Babe, who hath retrieved our loss,
From his poor manger to his bitter cross;
Then we may hope, the angelic host among,
To sing, redeemed, a glad triumphal song.

John Byrom

FOR FURTHER READING

The reader who is interested in following up the ideas developed in this work will find the following useful.

For Luther's 'theology of the cross', and the background against which it developed, see:

Walther von Loewenich, *Luther's Theology of the Cross* (Belfast: Christian Journals, 1976)

Alister E. McGrath, *Luther's Theology of the Cross: Martin Luther's Theological Breakthrough* (Oxford: Blackwell, 1985).

For the use of this theology in modern German Christology, see:

Jürgen Moltmann, *The Crucified God: The Cross as the Foundation and Criticism of Christian Theology* (London: SCM, 1974)

Eberhard Jüngel, *God as the Mystery of the World: On the Foundation of the Theology of the Crucified One in the Dispute between Theism and Atheism* (Edinburgh: T. & T. Clark, 1983).

Jüngel's book is particularly difficult reading. For an introduction to both these works, and the background against which they were written, see:

Alister McGrath, *The Making of Modern German Christology: From the Enlightenment to Pannenberg* (Oxford: Blackwell, 1986).

For more general studies of the relevance of the crucifixion and resurrection to the Christian faith, see:

John Stott, *The Cross of Christ* (Leicester: IVP, 1986)

Alister McGrath, *Understanding Jesus: Who Jesus is and why he matters* (Eastbourne: Kingsway, 1987)

George Carey, *The Gate of Glory* (London: Hodder & Stoughton, 1986).

For further discussion of the relevance of these ideas to the life of the church, particularly in relation to contemporary culture, see the following two important studies:

Lesslie Newbigin, *The Other Side of 1984: Questions for the Churches* (Geneva: WCC, 1983)

Lesslie Newbigin, *Foolishness to the Greeks: The Gospel and Western Culture* (London: SPCK, 1986).